Presented to

_____

From

_____

Date

_____

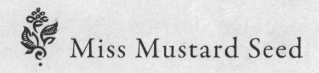

Miss Mustard Seed

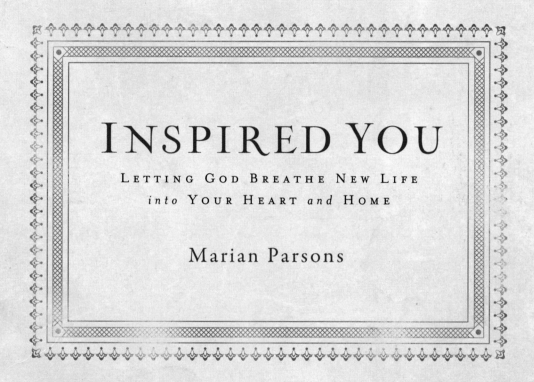

INSPIRED YOU

LETTING GOD BREATHE NEW LIFE
into YOUR HEART *and* HOME

Marian Parsons

THOMAS NELSON
Since 1798

NASHVILLE   DALLAS   MEXICO CITY   RIO DE JANEIRO

Please use caution and common sense when working on DIY projects. Always follow manufacturers' instructions and wear the appropriate safety gear, especially when using power tools. Old paint and finishes may contain lead, so take the necessary measures to keep you and your family safe. For detailed information, visit http://www.epa.gov/lead/.

For . . .

. . . my husband, who loves me because of my

desire to create and decorate, not in spite of it.

. . . my boys, who make messes

but bring so much joy to my life.

. . . and my parents, who encouraged me to take a chance.

ACKNOWLEDGMENTS

S O MANY WONDERFUL PEOPLE have supported me through this journey of writing my first book. I would like to specifically thank: My family, of course, for all of their love.

The gift book team at Thomas Nelson, for seeing my potential and making this book a reality.

My editor, Michelle Prater Burke, for bringing out the best in my words and photographs.

Charlene Mindte, aka "Mini Mustard Seed," for taking such great care of Marshall and Calvin when I needed to work and for being my hand model.

Jami Clune, Dee Kasberger, Lisa Leonard, Laura Dreyer, Cindy Austin, Ann Drake, Kristi Abernathy, Alice and Jay, and Christi Wilson for creating some of the beautiful accessories, artwork, and pillows in my home.

Karen Watson, Barb Blair, Shaunna West, Donna Williams, and all of the "DIY Divas" for their friendship, advice, and encouragement.

Jody McKitrick for taking beautiful photos of me for this book.

All of my blog readers, fans, and friends for following my adventures through every blog post. This book may not have happened without their subscriptions, comments, and clicks.

Last, but certainly not least, I am so thankful to the Lord for creating me, saving me, shaping me into who I am today, and using me despite all my imperfections.

CONTENTS

1. The Inspired You............................... 11

2. Breathing New Life into Your Home............ 27

3. The Imperfect, Everyday Home................. 49

4. The Treasure Hunt............................ 73

5. Making Things New 101

6. Creating a Handmade Home................... 131

7. Decorating Dollars and Sense................. 153

8. Inspired Entertaining......................... 183

9. Finding Contentment 205

10. If Walls Could Talk 225

Chapter 1

THE INSPIRED YOU

SOME GIRLS GET GIDDY over a new pair of shoes or an outfit that redefines their image. I get giddy over room makeovers. And finding an amazing piece of furniture at a yard sale. And sewing curtains from scratch. Shall I go on? I can't help it. I love every aspect of it. With a little bit of work, time, and money, an entire home can be transformed into a beautiful space.

When my enthusiasm and passion for decorating bubbles over in a conversation, I often get a response like, "I wish I knew how to decorate. I don't really have a flair for that kind of thing." The idea that you're either good at creating a beautiful home or you aren't seems to be prevalent today. We're constantly bombarded with images of gorgeous rooms in shelter magazines, on TV, and all over the home-decorating blog world. It's easy to feel like everyone is good at it but you. Like everyone is living in an "after space" and you're sitting around in your "before," hoping a celebrity designer with a crew and a truck full of sweet furniture will show up on your doorstep to do a complete home makeover.

Beautiful homes start with inspiration and a willingness to try.

I am not denying that it would be awesome for that crew to swoop in and create a dream home in three days (and you then get to cry tears of joy about it on national television), but there is so much satisfaction and self-discovery (some tears as well) that come when *you* transform your home. No need to look back over your shoulder. I'm talking to you. *You* can create a beautiful home. Now, don't start rattling off excuses about your failed attempts at sewing in middle-school home economics or think things like, *I'm not a creative person.* You *can* create a beautiful home. It doesn't matter if you're right-brained, left-brained, type A, or whatever. Think of it this way: God is the creator of all things, and we are made in His image, so surely there is a creative side to all of us. Working on your home might be the best way to bring out that creativity.

Let's now redefine what a beautiful home is. It's not about big budgets and magazine-quality perfection; it's about making the best of what you have and finding contentment despite what you don't. It's not about keeping up with the hottest trends, style setters, or the neighbors; it's about creating a space that feels inviting, is functional for your family, and shows off the style and interests of the people who live there. When boiled down, that's it. Doesn't that seem like a more achievable standard? You don't need a huge budget, a degree in interior design, or a boatload of DIY (do-it-yourself) experience. You don't need to start with a dream home. Your journey can start today, with what you already know, what you have, and whatever time your schedule allows.

So let's not waste any time and dive right into a project. Do you have a frame? Any frame. Big, small, any finish, missing the glass, whatever. With a frame and a few inexpensive supplies from the hardware store, you can make your very own custom chalkboard.

Chalkboard Tutorial

I love using chalkboards in decorating. They're playful yet classic as well. I use them to display poems, verses, songs, menus, or just doodles. Choose a gold leaf frame for a formal look, warm wood for a classic style, or a brightly painted lacquer frame for a modern take.

What you'll need:

- A picture frame
- A piece of hardboard or Masonite cut to fit inside the picture frame
- Chalkboard spray paint
- Chalk
- A hammer and small nails

Step 1: Paint Chalkboard

Using long, smooth strokes, spray the smooth side of the hardboard or Masonite with chalkboard spray paint. Apply two or three coats, allowing ample drying time between coats.

Step 2: Season Chalkboard

Once paint is completely dry, rub a piece of chalk over the entire surface. This will season the chalkboard and ensure that writing isn't "burned" into the surface. For a clean look, wipe chalkboard with a wet paper towel. For a vintage look, use a dry paper towel.

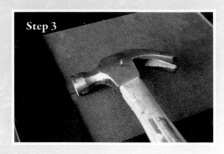

Step 3

Step 3: Assemble Chalkboard

Insert hardboard into frame. If needed, secure in place with some small nails. Hang or lean chalkboard to use.

. . . .

Tip: Most hardware stores will cut pieces of wood to size for you if you don't have a saw at home. If you don't want to spend the money on a piece of Masonite, stiff cardboard or any sturdy, flat, paintable surface can be used. I've even painted the back side of a mirror with chalkboard paint before!

. . . .

This may be one small project, but that's how beautiful homes are created. It starts with inspiration and a willingness to try. Then an "after" home is built one project at a time, one skill at a time, one purchase at a time. It's a process—one that is rewarding, fun, and a bit addictive, and one that can bring out talents and abilities you never knew you had.

LOSING AND FINDING
THE INSPIRED ME

I have always found joy in creative endeavors. I was singing in church at the age of four, and I pursued theater, dance, and music all the way through college. I developed a love of interior design as a "military brat" while my dad was stationed in Germany. Touring castles and staying in quaint guesthouses were fuel for my creative eye. Rearranging the furniture in my dollhouse as a young girl turned into sketching elaborate house plans on graph paper when I was in middle school. When my husband, Jeff, and I were finally able to purchase our first home, the decorating floodgates were opened. I painted every surface of that town house (some more than once), took on several DIY projects, and loved every minute of it. I started dreaming about what our next house would be like and what projects would be waiting for us there.

Then we moved to a new town, bought a home, and had two baby boys, Marshall and Calvin, all within about a two-year period. You may have guessed, and rightly so, that most DIY projects I had been dreaming about were shelved (although I did refinish our floors when I was five months pregnant, but that's another totally ridiculous story I'll get to later). As a stay-at-home mom, my day was filled with grocery shopping, cooking, cleaning, dropping kids off, picking kids up, picking toys up, putting kids in time-out, taking the trash out, emptying the dishwasher . . . and on it went. Day after day. I find great joy in homemaking and motherhood as a whole (I guess I could do without the laundry and

cleaning toilets), but there came a time when I was sitting on my sofa with a four-month-old and an almost two-year-old, and I felt totally overwhelmed.

I remember the morning vividly. I was sitting on my sofa, in sweatpants, of course, and the endless parade of diapers, dishes, laundry (ugh), and bills was suffocating me. My mom called and probably asked a simple question like, "How is your day going?" Questions like that are dangerous when they're directed at someone who is just a question away from bursting into tears. The end result was just that—me bursting into tears. I had reached that moment in my life when I realized I wasn't thriving. I was just churning through the routine of my day. As I was trying to articulate this to my mom between sobs, she stopped me. "Marian, I've been saying for a while now that you should start your own creative business. Maybe this is the time to step out and do just that."

I knew she was right, but I had always thought that starting my own business was something I would talk about and never really do. Dozens of reasons prevented me from giving it serious consideration. I didn't know anything about taxes or insurance. I wasn't a "business-minded" person. I lacked the formal training. I also didn't have the money. The reasons I spewed out did not deter my mom: "Give it a try. Go for it, and we'll help."

I remember pausing as I digested those words. *Could I really do it? Do people like me just decide one day to start a business?* I felt hope. Starting my own business was a way I could achieve two goals: stay at home with my young boys and, hopefully, contribute to the household income. It even fulfilled a third intangible goal I never expected—an outlet for my creativity and a way to pursue my passion for decorating. I wiped away the tears and immediately started writing down ideas. I talked it over with Jeff, and the work began.

Starting that countertop business was exactly what I needed, and God used it to pull me out of my funk. I relished the creative process and the fact that I could shop at yard sales, make over pieces of furniture, and decorate my home as a part of my business. Even though I was working harder than ever, I had more energy than ever. I was up late at night, refinishing a dresser to sell or making a slipcover for my family room, but I didn't mind waking up at 6:00 a.m. to the chubby hand of a toddler pulling at my pajama sleeve to rouse me from my bed. The mountains of laundry (my favorite), sticky floors, and smashed crackers were all still there and a part of my daily life, but I didn't feel like I was drowning in it anymore. I felt inspired again. And believe it or not, you can too. My mom gave me a little push to start using my creative talents, and I have been so blessed because of it. This book may be the little push you need.

START CREATING A BEAUTIFUL HOME (LIKE, RIGHT NOW!)

If you're surrounded by 1980s wallpaper sporting geese with bonnets or you've cried tears over the avocado-green bathtub, sink, and matching toilet that you just can't afford to replace right now, you might snicker (or cry harder) at the

thought of making that space beautiful. I know there are challenging rooms out there, and I'm sure you have limitations. It's pretty rare to have all the time, money, and skills required to turn every square foot into all your heart desires. No matter what your situation, though, today is a good day to start, and there is always something you can do to improve your space, even if it's just a little at a time. (And I'm not suggesting you "improve" that avocado bathroom by taking a sledgehammer to it before your spouse gets home from work today, however tempting it might be.)

When Jeff and I first moved into our current house, we were ready to

get to work to make it exactly what we wanted it to be, but there were two big problems . . . time and money. I was six months pregnant with our first son when we moved in, and I wanted the entire house renovated in a week. In other words, I was in major nesting mode. The second issue was money. Our budget was, like, zero. Does that sound familiar to anyone? I'm guessing it does. Remember that I had been dreaming about everything I was going to do to this house, so a lack of time and money and an overabundance of hormones (a volatile combination) were not enough to stop me from making some immediate improvements. So I figured out a few steps anyone can take to make the greatest impact in a home right away and on a shoestring:

- **Clean it**. I know this step isn't the most exciting, but it works. A clean home looks beautiful, plus it's more comfortable and inviting. Clean the windows, give dusty blinds a bath, shampoo the carpet, and get all the dead bugs out of your ceiling light fixtures. (Come on, we all have those!) Take it to the next level by making the beds, clearing away the clutter, and straightening things up. You will be surprised how much a thorough cleaning and some "fluffing" will transform a space.
- **Remove what you don't like**. That's what we did with the Berber carpeting that was covering the original hardwood floors in our house. We didn't have the money to refinish the floors right away, but we could remove the stained and stinky carpet, which immediately improved the room. Don't go overboard with this, though. If you hate your hand-me-down couch but it's the only place your family has to sit, don't set it out by the curb until you have a replacement. Move out the accessories and

furniture you don't use and don't like. It's better to have a sparse room furnished with a few things you love than a room stuffed with things you don't like.

- **Rearrange the furniture**. I like to call this "resetting a room." Take everything out except the large pieces of furniture you know you want to keep. Get a friend or family member to help you scoot the furniture around the room until you find the best arrangement. Put in pictures and accessories, and try new arrangements. This is a great thing to do with the change of the seasons, just to keep things fresh and to incorporate new holiday decor.

- **Shop your house**. Pull furniture and accessories from other areas of the house to try in new rooms. You probably have a lot of things sitting around that would look great if repurposed or simply put in a new place. I once cut a bed pillow in half and stitched each raw end because I needed two pillows for a pair of side chairs. Voilà! Two accent pillows out of one unused bed pillow. Put your ingenuity to work and give it a try, even if your idea sounds a little nutty.

- **Swap with a friend or family member**. Most people have hand-me-down furniture or things they bought a long time ago that they no longer love. Try to arrange a swap where you can put items from your home up for grabs and your friends and family can do the same. You may end up with some pieces you really love, and you can bring an entirely new look to your home (and theirs) for free.

- **Shop the curb**. Go ahead and get the giggles out about curb shopping and Dumpster diving. I know it sounds gross, but I'm serious. Some people throw away very nice things, and there's no reason to let them go to a landfill. I once found a caned French settee on the side of the road. I asked Jeff to turn around so I could rescue it. The back leg was broken, but he was able to fix that for me, and I used it in my house for about four years. Just make sure you're taking something that was meant for the trash and not a piece someone is loading into his vehicle. It's a good idea to knock on the door and ask permission before claiming your discovery as your own. Also, there are often "curb alerts" and free listings on sites such as Craigslist and Freecycle.

Put your ingenuity to work, even if your idea sounds a little nutty.

I hope these ideas have given you a starting point on the journey of transforming your house into a home you love. Are you feeling inspired yet?

DISCOVERING THE INSPIRED YOU

Perhaps you're in that place, that same wallowing-in-self-pity place I was in a few years ago, or you're just churning through the daily routine of your life. You might be able to concede that you could have untapped creative talents or possibly some mad furniture refinishing skills, but you're too drained and uninspired at the end of the day to test them out. You go to bed feeling like it's a victory that your house doesn't look like it belongs on an episode of *Hoarders*. Well, it's time to get out of survival mode and start thriving.

> *It's time to get out of survival mode and start thriving.*

Working on your home is a great way to unearth hidden abilities or rediscover ones that have gotten a little dusty while you raised your family or worked long hours in an office. God has given you talents for a reason—so you can feel fulfilled *using* them and then share them with others. Putting your gifts to good use will bring so much joy to your life, and that joy will be evident to your family and friends. It's hard to hide the immense satisfaction you can experience when you make a slipcover for the lumpy, faded recliner you inherited from your bachelor uncle. You'll ooze excitement over a headboard you made with big-girl tools all by yourself. (Oh yes.) And while you're experiencing that creative spark, the reward of a job well done, and the intense joy of a tidy space, you'll also be creating a beautiful and inviting space for you, your family, and all who enter your home as a big bonus. As God breathes new life into your heart, it will spill over into your home. And that's so much better than the instant gratification you'd get with a TV makeover. ❦

Chapter 2

BREATHING NEW LIFE
INTO YOUR HOME

I MOVED A LOT AS A KID. I didn't view this as the ruin of my primary school social life, but as a great adventure. For my mom, however, it was . . . well, an adventure of another kind. When we moved to our military housing in Stuttgart, Germany, she cried. When we moved into the house my dad purchased in Virginia, she cried. In both of those places, she faced something a lot of us face: trying to make a beautiful home out of a house we don't really like. As a kid, I was baffled by her tears. I just cared about who got the bigger bedroom, and I didn't notice the army-green counters, purple walls, and hideous flooring that were all so distressing to my mom. "There she goes! Mom's crying about the house . . . again." As an adult, I've come to understand her tears.

Most women make an emotional investment in a home. Call it nesting or maternal instincts; it's there, and it can be fierce. We want a place for our family to live that's comfortable, warm, welcoming, and beautiful. In both Germany and Virginia, my mom walked through the front door and was overwhelmed by the "before" state of those spaces. Some of you may have had similar experiences. Maybe you're still looking around your house, wondering how you can ever be content living there. Where do you even begin?

Most women make an emotional investment in a home. Call it nesting or maternal instincts; it's there, and it can be fierce.

Turning your befores into afters isn't only about the physical transformation; it's about the process. Long before the days of twenty-four-hour decorating shows on TV and shelter blogs, my mom figured out some innovative quick fixes to transform both of those spaces. She used quality contact paper that looked like butcher block to cover the hideous kitchen counters, and she starched a beautiful German fabric to an ugly metal divider in the bathroom. Although I always had dreams of living in a grand two-story Colonial instead (yes, I was a funny little kid), I never felt like my home was ugly or small. Without realizing it, my mom was building something more important than a pretty space. She was building *me*. She could've raised the white flag and decided that if it wasn't her dream home, it wasn't worth the effort. But it wasn't about whether the house was worth it; it was about her family, and *we* were worth it.

My mom showed me that there is a lot of potential in non-dream homes and that you can thrive wherever God puts you. This example would serve me well as my husband and I set out on our house hunt when we moved to Pennsylvania.

THE PERFECT HOME ISN'T ALWAYS A DREAM HOME

When my husband, Jeff, and I first set foot in our current home, it was not love at first sight. The house hunt had been an emotional and discouraging process. I had dreams of buying a quaint Pennsylvania farmhouse, but I quickly realized that was way out of our budget. All of the homes in our price range were not even close to what I had hoped for. One reeked of cigarette smoke and had a bizarre layout. One had a major mold issue in the basement and a bathtub that had been dyed blue. The worst of all was a farmhouse that was more than one hundred years old and, aside from siding and new windows (which I think were the only things keeping the house upright), it had not been touched in at least half a century. That would normally be a bonus in my book, but when I could actually see the sky through the roof, I knew I would be in over my head. Plus, Jeff wouldn't set foot in it, and that would be a major issue in itself. A couple of these homes had some great potential, but we could not afford the extensive renovations they would require.

When we finally looked at our home, the bar was pretty low. I was just praying for a non-dump that I could work with. The home we ended up purchasing fit the non-dump criterion and even went way beyond that low expectation. It

needed a lot of work, but it was work we could do at our own pace as we could afford it. It had quite a few bright spots as well. The original part of the home was built in 1948, and, aside from Berber carpet laid over the oak floors, it was relatively untouched. The lack of modernization might have been a negative for some buyers, but it was a big plus for me. Unlike the dilapidated farmhouse, this one had sturdy bones. I got the charm and history I longed for: pine doors with glass doorknobs, plaster walls, and sloped ceilings with cubbyhole closets and dormer windows. I knew I could turn this before home into an after, room by room.

TURNING YOUR BEFORES INTO AFTERS

I'm a little giddy right now. Room makeovers are on the horizon, and you remember how I feel about those—better than cute shoes. Seriously. I already offered some ideas in chapter 1 to jump-start your makeovers, and maybe that's all you needed. Sometimes decluttering and rearranging the furniture is all a space requires, and a clean canvas can get the creative wheels turning. But for some people and some perplexing spaces, a little more inspiration is required.

Using a few room transformations in my own house as examples, we'll walk through some high-style, minimal-cost ideas you can implement in your own rooms.

The Dining Room

What was wrong with the space—
Stained Berber carpet (over beautiful hardwood floors) and a 1980s ceiling fan. Enough said.

- Few things say "dining room" more clearly than a great chandelier. It doesn't have to be formal or traditional, but a well-selected light fixture can set the tone for the space. Depending on the height of your ceiling, a good rule of thumb is to leave 30 to 36 inches between your tabletop and the bottom of the chandelier.

- Dining room furniture doesn't have to be purchased in a matched set. In fact, I think it looks better if things don't match (it's also a lot cheaper!). I've paired antique farm chairs with a vintage French provincial table and matching arm chairs (see page 31). Just tie pieces together with color, size, finish, or style.

- I bought the bamboo mat in my dining room to use somewhere else, but when I slid it under the table on a whim, it really worked. It can be tricky to select a rug that works well in a room, so try a few different options, and your favorite may surprise you!

The Kitchen

What was wrong with the space—

Nothing. If you're dealing with 1980s laminate cabinets, powder-blue counters, or linoleum that's yellowed and wrinkled with age, you would hardly look at my "before" kitchen as a before. My kitchen is one of the things that sold me on this house. It's big, the layout is terrific, and I have oodles of storage and counter space. The finishes just weren't my taste. But it's okay to change parts of your home that were perfect choices for someone else, but not perfect for you. After all, it's *your* home!

What you can try in your house—

- Paint your cabinets. Short of a total gut job, few things are going to transform your kitchen more dramatically than painting the cabinets. Clean and degrease the cabinets prior to painting, use a quality bonding primer and give it two to three days to cure, then paint one to two coats of quality satin or semigloss oil or latex paint. Use quality brushes and foam rollers to keep the brushstrokes to a minimum. (Don't start painting your cabinets the day before your entire extended family comes to stay with you for Thanksgiving. This project takes several days and can make quite a mess.)

- Change out the hardware on your cabinets to give them a different look. A great place to buy unique knobs in bulk is eBay. If replacing all of the knobs is too costly, try spray painting them in a different finish.

- If a tile backsplash isn't in the budget, use chalkboard paint or bead board to add interest.

. . . .

Tip: If you'd like to jazz up your cabinets even more, top them off with crown moldings and use corbels underneath to add some bulk. Removing the doors, painting the interiors, and using the cabinets as open shelving is another way to totally transform the look.

. . . .

The Family Room

What was wrong with the space—

Again, this room had great bones, but the pinkish-beige color was off-putting, and the position and scale of the fireplace made a room arrangement tricky.

What you can try in your house—

- In chapter 1, we talked about removing things that don't work in a space, and that includes fireplaces. The one in our house wasn't functional, and it took up a huge amount of wall space, not to mention visual space. It dominated the room. Removing it freed up the wall for a buffet and flat-screen TV, which is much more practical for our family.

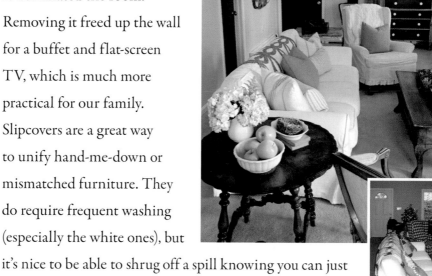

- Slipcovers are a great way to unify hand-me-down or mismatched furniture. They do require frequent washing (especially the white ones), but it's nice to be able to shrug off a spill knowing you can just throw the cushion cover in the washing machine.

- Paint interior doors an unexpected color. The doors in the addition of our house are painted in a charcoal gray, which looks a lot more interesting than builder-grade white.

The Home Office

What was wrong with the space—

Oh, goodness, where do I start? Between the patchwork floor, the gas pipe sticking up out of the floor, and the refrigerator wedged in a corner, there wasn't much right in this space. It was the original kitchen when the house was built in 1948, and the new kitchen made this space little more than a glorified hallway.

What you can try in your house—

- Built-in cabinetry is the perfect way to define a space and maximize function. If you don't have a woodworker handy, it's fairly simple to customize shelving units purchased from a store like Ikea to get the built-in look.
- Use similar or complementary colors and finishes in rooms that are joined. Because our home office connects the kitchen and dining room, it had to work well with both spaces. We used the same hardware and paint colors that were used for the kitchen cabinets and finished the floors to match those in the dining room.

The Living Room

What was wrong with the space—

Despite the room's beautiful light from south-facing windows, the pine trim made the room feel dark, and the dingy walls added to the dreariness. It also lacked overhead lighting, and one or two lamps weren't enough to fill the room with light.

What you can try in your home—

- Paint your walls a pale, neutral shade with a bright white ceiling and bright white trim. This is a classic combination that will look great in any home, any style, and any year.

- If you need some overhead lighting but don't want to pay an electrician to install a ceiling outlet (or have plaster walls as we do), purchase a kit to rewire a chandelier or wall sconces so that they can be plugged into a wall. I purchased two smaller chandeliers on clearance at a home store, painted and rewired them, and used a plastic cord cover to hide their cords where they ran along the wall. Paint the cord covers the same color as the wall and ceiling to provide additional camouflage.

. . . .

Tip: Most chandelier chains aren't very attractive, and they're very simple to cover with a custom sleeve. Cut a piece of fabric about 4 inches wide and twice as long as the length of the chain you want to cover. Fold the fabric in half lengthwise inside out and sew the edges together. You can even use fabric glue for a no-sew option. Turn the sleeve right-side out, and thread chain through it. For a chandelier that is already installed, you can hand stitch the sleeve around the chain instead.

. . . .

- Inject color and drama into the space by using bold curtain fabric. Simple floor-length panels look elegant and are simple to make.

Pleated Drapes Tutorial

I make all of my own curtains. I would have no problem buying them, but I can rarely find exactly what I'm looking for, and when I do find it, it costs way more than I want to spend. I usually make a simple sleeve drape, and although pleats may sound fancy and complicated, they are actually quite easy to make.

What you'll need for two floor-length panels:

- Two packs of 3⅞-inch four-prong drapery hooks (includes two end hooks)
- 3⅞-inch drapery pleater tape (about 6 yards for an average window)
- Approximately 6 yards of home decor fabric (54 inches wide)
- Sharp scissors
- Tape measure
- Sewing machine
- Pins
- Coordinating thread
- Iron and ironing board
- All-purpose sewing needle
- Curtain rod
- Curtain rings

Step 1: Measure and Cut Fabric

Hang curtain rod in desired place above the window. I prefer to hang my curtain rods a few inches higher and wider than the window to let in more light and make the window appear larger. Measure the height of the curtain rod with the tape measure. Measure and cut two fabric panels to the height of the curtain rod plus about 10 inches for seam and hem allowances.

Step 2

Step 2: Attach Header

Fold over top of the curtain about an inch and press along the fold. Place header tape just slightly under the curtain top. Use scissors to cut it 4 inches shorter than the curtain width. Pin pleater tape into place, leaving a 2-inch gap on both sides. The pleater tape has sleeves for later inserting the hooks. Make sure it's pinned so the sleeve openings are faceup and pointing down. Sew along the top and bottom of pleater tape to secure in place and remove pins. Repeat this process with the second curtain panel.

Step 3: Press and Sew Curtain Sides

Starting on one side, fold fabric over about an inch and press the fold down the entire length of the panel. Fold fabric over once more about an inch, so it overlaps the pleater tape, press with a hot iron, and pin into place. Repeat on the other side and then on both sides of the second curtain panel. Sew along pin lines with thread that coordinates with your fabric.

Step 3

Step 3

Step 4: Pleat Curtain

Here's where the magic of those hooks comes in! Starting at one end of the header, insert one end hook into the last sleeve. Skip two sleeves; then insert

 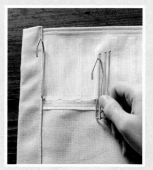  

the first four-prong hook. Then skip two more sleeves and insert the next four-prong hook. I like a deeper pleat, so I hook every other sleeve onto the four-prong hook. Continue this process for the width of the curtain header. Flip the curtain panel over so that the right side is facing up. Tack the bottom of each pleat in place with a needle and coordinating thread. Repeat with second curtain.

Step 4

Step 5: Hem Curtain

Slide curtain rings onto rod, hang hooks on curtain rings, and allow panel to hang freely. Fold panel up once and then a second time to create a hem. By hemming the drapes while they are on the rod, you can ensure they are the desired length. Drapes can either hang slightly off the floor, skim the floor, or pool on the floor, depending on the fabric and the desired look. Pin hem in place. Take drapes off of the rod and finish folding and pinning curtains to marked length.

Press hem and then sew along the top edge of the hem and down both sides. Remove pins and trim all loose threads. Hang your new pleated drapes by slipping the hooks through the curtain rings. Then enjoy having people ask where you bought them!

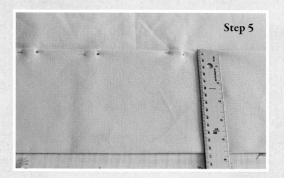

Step 5

Step 5

· ·

Tip: If you're working with larger windows, a good rule of thumb is to buy enough curtain fabric to run double the width of the window or the area you are covering. These drapes can also be hung from tracks to section off a room or to hide a storage or laundry area. I bought a fabric that looks good from both sides, so it didn't need to be lined, but you could certainly add a lining if you want. I use the bargain twin sheets from Walmart to line my curtains.

· ·

A DOSE OF REALITY

> *Homebuilding is an ongoing process, so don't let impatience overshadow the experience.*

Now that you've seen the "after" shots of some of the rooms in my house, I'll let you in on a little secret. They don't always look like that. I have two young kids, a husband, and teenagers from our church coming and going, so of course there are toys, crumbs, cups, spills, mail, papers, piles of laundry, and all of the stuff that comes with a busy family. Yes, it's hard to stay positive when you invest a lot of creativity and hard work in a space and then your family "messes it up." But remember, what's the point of a beautiful space if your family and guests can't enjoy it?

So, I don't want you to look at these finished, staged rooms and feel like your own spaces are inadequate. I'm not even showing you all of the rooms in my house because some just aren't finished yet. Also, these pictures show what my home looks like after more than five years of work. We lived with a lot of quick fixes before we were able to tackle some of the bigger projects like the office built-ins or the refinished floors, and big projects are still on the "to do" list. Homebuilding is an ongoing process, so don't let impatience overshadow the experience.

Growing up, I learned a lot from watching my mom beautify spaces that had brought her to tears when she had first seen them. Maybe you're in a similar situation. You feel defeated by the stained shag carpet, the industrial fluorescent lighting in your kitchen, or the inherited furniture that makes your home look like the set of a 1970s sitcom. Imagine what would happen if you—just

like my mom—decided to thrive wherever God put you. If your family saw those tears of despair turn into determination. If they saw you make the best of what you have to create the best home for them that you could. What a powerful example that could be and a wonderful way to build into your family. That's what breathing new life into your home is all about. 🌸

Chapter 3

THE IMPERFECT, EVERYDAY HOME

I HAVE A FAINT MEMORY of being messy when I was a child. My mom told me to clean my room, and I simply made pathways to the door, the bed, the dresser, and the closet. That was clean enough for me. When I hit sixth grade, though, something happened. After living in military housing all of my life, we finally moved into a real house (my mom cried over it, too, but it was a real house nonetheless), and I had a say in the decor of my room for the very first time ever. I became obsessively tidy and organized. I would actually flinch if someone sat on my bed and messed up the perfectly smoothed comforter or knocked my stuffed animals out of their arrangement. When I was in high school, I would decorate and redecorate my room and would even clean and straighten the entire house on occasion. My mom called me "the good-housekeeping fairy." This desire for domestic perfection only intensified as I got older, and it was fueled with glossy pages displaying perfect homes in decorating magazines and books. When Jeff and I finally bought our first house, it was a full-out obsession of mine to have a magazine-worthy home.

I'll take a minute to say that you should feel great sympathy for anyone who has to live in a house with someone obsessed with having a magazine-worthy home every second of the day. Oh, my poor husband. Jeff could hardly set down a glass of water before I would scoop it up, clean it, and put it away. Instead of creating a home about comfort, I created an unreasonable, unrealistic, and unfair environment that was all about looks. My priorities were way out of whack. Well, God has a sense of humor, and He knew exactly how to bring all of this to my attention . . . motherhood.

It is so easy to get preoccupied with our homes—and our lives—needing to be perfect or at least appearing that way.

Before I became pregnant with my first baby, I swore a bouncy seat would never, ever be in my house. I would use an antique cradle or just put the baby on a blanket. I was committed to my decorating ideal, and it did not include baby paraphernalia. As I started talking to veteran moms, however, it became clear that my expectations were ridiculous. I couldn't expect to have a baby in the house and not make changes to create a safe, comfortable, and fun environment for him. When we were blessed with our first son, I also quickly learned that I would be miserable if my highest priorities throughout the day were keeping the carpet spot-free and making sure the toys were put away. I would miss out on so many joys.

When I get in one of my "I-want-every-corner-of-my-home-to-look-like-a-magazine" frenzies, my priorities often get out of whack. I'm sure I'm not alone. (Please tell me I'm not alone!) Isn't it so easy to get preoccupied with our homes (and our lives) needing to be perfect or at least appearing that way? The idea of perfection is in our faces and shoved down our throats regularly in the form of images that have been edited to attain a level of perfection not possible in real life. This pursuit of impossible perfection can easily overshadow the things in life that *should* be more important, like our families and our faith. I have to remind myself (on many occasions) that there are more valuable pursuits than clutter-free counters, perfectly fluffed pillows, and spot-free slipcovers. It doesn't mean those things are wrong, but when that is *the* focus of my daily life, I've got a problem.

When we're striving for domestic perfection, we're missing the mark. If our highest priority is walking in faith and loving our families, we'll find joy in the sofa stains, the scratches on the dining room table, and the pile of shoes by the door. We'll be able to show love and grace when a child draws on the wall with a crayon or a husband leaves tools all over the counter. Most important, we will let the people in our lives know that we love them and that their mess doesn't take away from that.

> *If our highest priority is walking in faith and loving our families, we'll find joy in the sofa stains, the scratches on the dining room table, and the pile of shoes by the door.*

. . . .

Tip: If you find an overload of decorating books, magazines, and online sites are bringing out the green-eyed monster in you, walk away from them for a few days and focus on being thankful for what you have. Sometimes a short break is all we need to regain our perspective.

. . . .

BEHIND THE SCENES

I remember times when I've thumbed through a decorating book, looked around my room, let out a heavy sigh, and thought, *My space is never going to look that good*. I'm sure others can relate. When you see those pictures, though, remember that they are not an accurate representation of that house. You're seeing only the very best parts of the house. The area has been thoroughly cleaned, professionally staged, and photographed from the perfect angle with the best lighting scenario. Real-life items that are unsightly but necessary—like switch plates, cords, and smoke alarms—are edited out of the photos. Then the lighting, contrast, saturation, and clarity of the picture are adjusted to make the space look even better. How can your home or mine compete with that? They can't, and they don't need to.

Staged and Edited Photo   **Unedited Photo**   **Actual Living Photo**

On the previous page are three images that show what our home office looks like in a staged and edited photo, what the photo looks like unedited, and what the room looks like when we're actually living in it—and it can get much worse than this!

You might think that when I am working on a photo shoot, my house looks great, but it's usually a total mess. The furniture is moved all over, and accessories and pillows wait in line for their turn in the picture. It can take all day to get everything perfect. What you see is only what is in the frame, not the mess just to the left and the right. And when the photo shoot is over, I move everything back to where it was so that our house is livable again.

You and I don't buy decorating books so we can look at other people's messes. We turn to those books for inspiration.

But you and I don't buy decorating books so we can look at other people's messes. We can look at our own mess every day. We turn to those books for inspiration, creative stimulation, and ideas we can implement. The danger comes when we think our entire house has to look like that every minute of every day and that if it doesn't, we're not measuring up. Not only will that thought drive your family nutty, but it could also stir up discontentment within you. If you feel like you're not measuring up, I'd like to lovingly remind you that your worth is not found in the outward appearance of your house, but in the inward appearance of your heart.

There is a balance, though. We can't let our families live in filth, chaos, and total disarray. Providing our family with a clean, comfortable, and safe home is a way of taking care of them and showing them love. And we can do a lot in our homes to make the rooms more organized, functional, and beautiful. Those things just shouldn't be what's most important.

MAKING THE EVERYDAY BEAUTIFUL— ONE ROOM AT A TIME

Certain spaces in a home are magnets for clutter. By addressing those spaces and providing adequate and stylish storage options, you'll have a place for everything. And hopefully everything will be in its place. Most of the time. (It's not about twenty-four-hour perfection, right?)

. . . .

Tip: When undertaking the organization of a room or an entire house, don't feel like it has to be tackled all at once. Just work on one drawer or cabinet or tabletop or section of closet at a time until the room (and eventually your house) is organized. Setting reasonable goals that can be reached by allotting small amounts of time will greatly increase the likelihood of success.

. . . .

Foyer/Entry/Mudroom

Every home needs a place for the family to land. When we walk in the door, we're almost always carrying something, and that stuff needs a home. Dedicating a spot for backpacks, shoes, coats, purses, keys, loose change, and school papers will make a huge difference in the overall function and appearance of your home. And it's not just about having things look neat; it's also about being able to locate stuff when you're rushing out the door. I know many of us do not have the luxury of a dedicated mudroom, but you can create a mini mudroom almost anywhere.

- Find an oversized lidded basket to hold shoes and backpacks.
- Use a pretty ironstone bowl to hold keys and loose change.
- Install a row of sturdy hooks by the door for coats and bags.
- Use a chest or trunk as a nice home for bags and shoes as well as a place to sit when putting them on.
- Corral boots in a large metal tray during the winter and rainy seasons.
- Convert a freestanding armoire or wardrobe into a mini mudroom. Install a bar for hanging coats; insert baskets for gloves, hats, and scarves; and label cubbies or drawers for shoes and bags.

Living Room/Family Room

The main living area can get out of control fast, especially if kids are in the house. My family definitely spends the bulk of our time in this room—watching TV, playing games, building cushion forts, wrestling, and cuddling up for movie nights. We need storage for toys, video games, movies, and the thirty-seven (okay, it's only eight) remote controls needed to operate all of our electronics. In this room, comfort is crucial. It also needs to be versatile. The furniture has to be easily moved for active video games, and extra seating is needed when we have teenagers over from our church. Family rooms are hardworking spaces but very public spaces as well, so we want them to meet all needs while looking nice.

Find pieces that provide lots of storage but leave a small footprint. Taller cabinets and hutches will take up a small amount of floor space but can hold a lot. I found this antique stepback cupboard (see next page) at a junk shop for around

$200. The upper cabinet allows for display space while the lower cabinet provides closed storage for building blocks and craft supplies.

Vintage buffets and dressers can be great stand-ins for TV consoles. Look for a piece that allows for easy access to movies and video games and also has room for TV components. Drawers can simply be removed so a component can fit inside. Drill a large hole in the back for cords and ventilation.

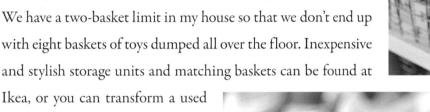

A shelf with baskets keeps toys accessible for kids but out of the way. I think this storage method is much more practical than a large lidded basket simply because it's easier for kids to see their toys. It also minimizes the number of toys out at one time. We have a two-basket limit in my house so that we don't end up with eight baskets of toys dumped all over the floor. Inexpensive and stylish storage units and matching baskets can be found at Ikea, or you can transform a used bookcase with paint, trim, casters, and vintage locker baskets.

I love antique tool caddies for the warm patina of the wood or the perfectly chipped paint, but I also love how practical they are for stylish storage. I purchased this one at an antique store for $28 and use it to hold all of our remote controls.

Place a basket by a favorite reading spot as a place to put magazines, newspapers, or puzzle books. Go through the basket every few weeks to clean out the old publications and make room for new ones.

An old garden caddy holds crayons on our coffee table next to a vintage wire tray filled with activity books. When two mismatched wooden chairs are pulled up to the table, it makes a space that encourages my boys to sit down and draw. Even if you don't have children in your home all the time, this is a great setup to keep visiting kids entertained while adults are chatting.

A small dresser or desk is an ideal place to store bills or craft supplies if you don't have a separate office or craft space. Look for pieces that are multifunctional and provide lots of storage.

Ultimately, I feel like the family room is one of those rooms you just have to "go with" or go crazy. Some of you may have the luxury of a bonus room or playroom, so your oversized recliners, sports-themed fleece blankets, treadmills, and stacks of magazines might have another home; but for a good number of us, this room is it, and that's okay. Remember how I was never going to have a bouncy seat in my house? Well, I not only ended up with a bouncy seat but also a Jumperoo, ExerSaucer, walker, and—for good measure—play gym. It was a bit of a struggle for me to overlook all of the primary colors, loud patterns, and blinking lights at times, but the baby and toddler years go by so quickly. Then all of the gear can be passed along to the next family expecting a bundle of joy. So don't get bent out of shape about those things. Enjoy each stage of growth in your family—and all of the stuff that may come with it.

Kitchen

I have learned that kitchen counters are the biggest magnet for stuff, so it's a challenging room to keep organized. (We should have a contest for the strangest thing found on a kitchen counter. *How does some of that stuff get there?*) But I've also learned that few things make my house look better than when I clear

off the counters and wipe them down. There's something about clean and clutter-free countertops that makes a space look amazing, especially if your home has an open floor plan.

If you have limited cabinet and counter space, install a pot rack for pots, pans, strainers, and stainless steel or copper bowls. It gives the kitchen a gourmet look and frees up a lot of space.

Dry goods like flour, sugar, oatmeal, pasta, cereals, and snacks can be stored in large glass canisters on a counter. Add clever labels to each jar for a personal touch.

A large tray or platter can be used to contain several smaller objects like a bottle of olive oil, a salt crock, and a mortar and pestle. The entire tray can be moved for cleaning or if the counter space is needed.

Add some character to your kitchen by using unique containers to hold frequently used objects. I use a 1903 relay race trophy found in my grandfather's attic to hold my kitchen utensils. I also keep vitamins in a vintage card catalog and fruit in an antique peanut scale.

After struggling with a paper towel holder that fell over almost daily for a few years, I finally gave up and stored several rolls in an antique fish basket. As an added bonus, I find that I don't have to run down to the basement to fetch another roll of paper towels every other day (even if the extra exercise was a good thing).

Office or Craft Room

Storage is key in an office or craft room. I have three large antique armoires in my work office to house all of my decorating books, fabric, craft supplies, and photography equipment. Built-ins, bookcases, shelving units, and hutches are all great options for maximizing your storage.

Pretty creamers and petite pitchers are a stylish way to store scissors and brushes.

I use a vintage test tube rack as a holder for my pens and pencils. A wire or glass floral frog is also a clever, inexpensive option and looks better than anything you can find in an office supply store.

Wire, rattan, and metal baskets are a convenient way to sort bills, mail, and paperwork or keep essential tools and supplies on hand.

Personalize a standard office chair with a simple slipcover, or find a second-hand chair that suits your personality and style.

A growing trend in styling bookcases is placing books on shelving with the spine facing inward so that you only see the neutral pages. (Jeff does not understand this.) I love the look of it and use it in my own home, but only with books we don't read often or use as a resource. A better option for those books is to arrange them by color so the titles are visible and the book jackets aren't competing with the overall aesthetic of the room. Another possibility, which

is time-consuming but inexpensive, is to cover the books in brown craft paper,

vellum, or scrapbook paper and label each book by hand. I love this look as well,

but I've never had the patience to sit down and do it.

Bedrooms

A bedroom should be a sanctuary and a refuge. For children, it should be a place of rest and wonder. For guests, it should be a place of comfort away from home. However, bedrooms are often places where we put our castoffs, let our laundry pile up, and "never get around to" decorating. (Are you picking up on my feelings about laundry yet?)

Side tables are an easy way to make someone happy. I'm serious! If ever I'm without a nightstand, I get bent out of shape. Where do I put my glasses, cup of water, or the clip I took out of my hair? A well-thought-out nightstand can provide additional storage in a bedroom and definitely increases the comfort factor. A small dresser or buffet, a washstand, or a petite cabinet are perfect options for side tables. A kitchen stool, plant stand, or corbel mounted on the wall can stand in for a nightstand in a tiny space.

Bedrooms look their best when the bed is made, so don't create a pillow-scape that requires a photographic memory to re-create each morning. I've done that, and it's stressful for a spouse or guest to try to figure out how to put your pillow-puzzle back together. Keep it pretty, simple, and most of all, comfortable. My boys are young, so I just use a flat sheet and a couple of blankets so that it's very simple for them to make their beds (when they do).

Task lighting is essential in a bedroom. Most people like to read in bed or at least have a light close by that can be easily turned on and off. Hang wall-mounted lights or set a lamp on the nightstand to provide that task lighting.

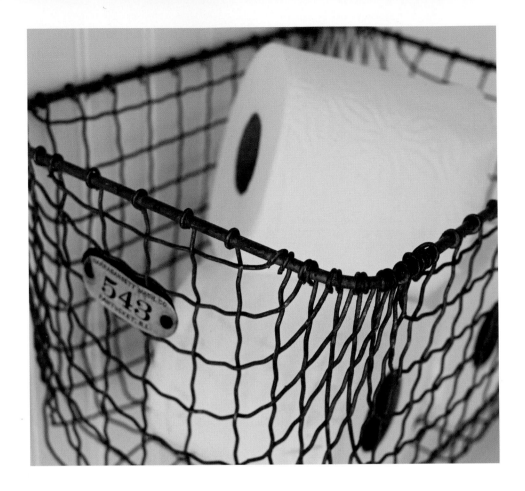

Bathrooms

Bathrooms are all about function. In recent years, though, magazines and decorating shows have convinced us that we need to have a spa in our homes and that it's impossible for two people to share a sink. Although I certainly wouldn't turn down a spa-like bathroom, it's just not necessary. Small touches can be added to an ordinary bathroom to make this functional space pretty and even luxurious.

Hooks are one of my favorite pieces of bathroom hardware. I've never been a big fan of towel bars. They seem like a convenience, but it's almost impossible to use a towel and then fold it and smooth it out over the bar so it looks presentable. Who wants rumpled, wet towels hanging on the bar or perfectly folded ones that have a layer of dust along the top because no one is allowed to touch them? I finally gave up on that effort altogether and opted for hooks on the back of each bathroom door. It's much more functional, and there is something charming and nostalgic about a row of hooks.

Toiletries do not have to be hidden in medicine cabinets. Store swabs and cotton balls in glass apothecaries. Bars of soap can be kept at the ready in a canister, and stores of toilet paper can be held in a basket or crate. I also like using small pitchers or crocks to hold toothbrushes.

A pretty shower curtain can do a lot for a bathroom. It creates closed storage in the tub so shampoo bottles and bath toys aren't on display for all to see. It's also a way to add softness, color, and texture to a room that can be stark.

If a bathroom is large enough, a freestanding piece of furniture provides additional storage and can bring character to the space. Look for a piece that will add vertical storage without taking up a lot of floor space. In a small room, try hanging a shelf or cabinet.

Keep accessories very simple and make sure they don't interfere with the function of the space.

············· · · ·

THE RIGHT KIND OF PERFECTION

We've established that our homes don't have to be magazine material to be special, beautiful, and inviting, and there are ways we can decorate around everyday life. Notice I'm not saying to work our lives around the decor. (I've tried that, and it's ridiculous.) As you start to implement some of these ideas, observe how your family lives in each space. Then figure out how best to decorate around their daily activities. Include everyone in the process, so the entire family knows where everything belongs and the room is functional for each of them. Make sure to be flexible. I can't tell you how many times I thought I had come up with the perfect solution only to find out it was totally impractical. If something's not working, let it go and work toward another idea that will be more functional. This sort of compromise has challenged my creativity and resourcefulness, and I usually end up liking the new idea better than the original.

Our homes don't have to be magazine material to be special, beautiful, and inviting.

All the ideas I've shared are simply that—ideas. And they may not work in every household. You may copy these ideas exactly or use them as a jumping-off point for your own innovative solutions. Every family's needs are different, and a creative magazine caddy for one could result in nothing but stubbed toes for another. Fight those urges to make everything perfect, and focus on making your home perfect for *your* family and guests. That's the kind of perfection that is worth striving for. ❧

Chapter 4

THE TREASURE HUNT

I AM AN AVID YARD SALER. You may be familiar with *that type*. We wake up early each Saturday morning, stop at the ATM for cash, and set out in anticipation of what we might find that day. We get flush in the face at the sight of a thrift store. We turn on a dime when we see a fluorescent poster-board sign. We don't mind wading through racks of musty clothes, antiquated electronics, and used shoes to get to the good stuff. And when we find the treasure we weren't looking for but knew we wanted the instant we saw it, we relish the victory. If you're *one of those*, you get it. If you're not, you may be intrigued and a little grossed out at the thought of shopping second-hand. (And you probably hate driving behind us when we're looking for yard sales.)

I do get some raised eyebrows from friends and acquaintances who don't understand it at all. How can I be giddy about a piece of furniture that's scratched and missing a drawer? How can I be over the moon about a pair of curvy chairs with furry green upholstery? On an outing a few years ago, I was delighted to find a stack of ironstone plates for practically nothing at a church yard sale. The gentleman handling the money looked at me, then looked at the old dishes, and then proceeded to point out the stacks of nicer, newer dishes they had for sale. He didn't get it. I happily paid for my chipped and cracked dishes and went on my way.

I couldn't tell you the exact moment it started. I remember going to yard sales on occasion with my mom when I was little, and it was even cool at my high school to scour thrift stores for vintage or brand-name clothing. (Or maybe I was a dork and thought it was cool?) When I was a newlywed in our first apartment, buying secondhand was the only option that fit my budget. Well, I could buy a cheapo piece of pressboard furniture, or I could buy a solid wood antique that needed some work. I chose the latter, and that shopping method stuck. I haven't bought pressboard since. Even if I had thousands of dollars to spend on the furnishings and decor in my house, I would hit the flea markets, antique stores, and auctions before I set foot in a mall.

DISCOVERING POTENTIAL

I want to challenge you to start looking at things—and people and situations—for what they can be, not what they are.

Shopping secondhand has a lot of benefits—it's the ultimate way to recycle, it's budget friendly, and it's fun not knowing what you'll find. When I take my sons out with me, I tell them that we're hunting for treasures. Secondhand shopping also hones your ability to see something that others may not—potential. The ability to see something not for what it is but instead for what it *can* be is a great gift. If I went to a furniture store and bought the five-piece furniture set with matching lamps for each room in my house, it wouldn't really be worth mentioning or writing a book about. If I piece together hand-me-downs and thrifted finds, reinvent them, and create a beautiful space, well, that's something special. I want to challenge you to start looking at things—and people and situations—for what they can be, not what they are. I think you'll find treasures in all aspects of your life, treasures that have been hiding right under your nose.

WHEN A BARGAIN ISN'T A BARGAIN

You have no idea how excited I was when I found Proverbs 31:18: "She watches for bargains." That's me! I love watching, hunting, looking, scouring, or whatever for a good bargain. It's not only a hobby and now a part of my business, but it also makes me a virtuous woman. (I have to make sure I point that out to Jeff.) I'm being a bit facetious, but there it is in the Bible.

There is a difference, though, between buying a bargain because it's a great deal and buying something you love, need, or want that happens to be a great bargain. I was once in one of my favorite antique malls and saw a woman pushing around a cart full of odds and ends. She looked at me, slouched over her cart, and sighed. "These are all just such great bargains, I couldn't pass them up," she said. I looked at her. "What are you going to do with all of them?" She sighed again and slouched lower as if the cart were weighing her down. "I don't know. I just can't pass them

> *Sometimes we need to spread the joy of bargains around and pass them up for other people to find.*

up." She shuffled along, hunting for more bargains she couldn't pass up. In my early days of shopping, I felt like that. I would find some cute thing at a yard sale for $1. *Only $1!* But I didn't love it. I didn't need it. I wasn't going to use it. But it was such a great bargain; how could I pass it up? I ended up surrounded by things I didn't love, didn't need, and didn't use. Some bargain.

I finally changed my approach. I decided I would run through a list of questions before getting excited about a low price tag. When something catches my eye, I go through this list: Do I love it? Do I need it? (Or, in my case, can I sell it

and make a profit on it?) Will I use it? If the answer is yes to any of these questions, it's okay for me to buy it if it's in my budget. If the answer is no to all of those, I don't buy it, even if it's a great bargain. I've trained myself to think, *That's a great bargain, and someone else is going to be really excited about it.* Sometimes we need to spread the joy of bargains around and pass them up for other people to find.

My favorite places to watch for bargains are antique/junk shops, yard sales, flea markets/antique fairs, thrift stores, online classified ads, and auctions. I'm going to share all my tips to help you see potential that others may not see so you can shop these venues like a pro.

Shopping Antique Stores

If you've never shopped at antique stores, the first thing you need to know is not all antique stores are alike. Some are very high-end with museum-quality antiques. Then there are antique malls or co-ops where a collection of dealers offer a lot of variety and a range of prices and styles. Junk shops are the places where you have to dig through dusty, cobweb-covered piles and feel like you need to go home and take a shower afterward. The second two varieties are my favorite to frequent.

Learn the ropes. Shopping for antiques as a novice can be overwhelming. I remember when I first set foot in an antique store and left feeling totally lost. I knew I loved antiques, but I wasn't sure if something was a good bargain or even what my style was and how antiques would fit into it. It took me a while to find my bearings. Be patient with yourself as you learn. Try shopping with a friend who can offer some wisdom.

Buy what you love. There is *a lot* out there. You have decades of decor to choose from. Just buy what you're drawn to and what you love. The way all of those pieces work together, however unconventional, is your unique style.

Don't get bamboozled. Just because something's in an antique store doesn't mean it's an antique. It's okay to buy reproductions (and there are very convincing ones out there). Just make sure you know what you're buying so you're not disappointed later. (I once bought a cake stand at an antique mall and was totally deflated when I found it for half the cost at Walmart.)

It's not all about value. Unless you're an antique dealer or want to resell what you're buying, don't buy pieces strictly as an investment. This guideline doesn't apply in all cases, but for the average antiquer, it's a good rule to follow. Buy what you love, and if it ends up being a great investment, that's just a bonus.

Firm or negotiable? Most prices on antiques are negotiable, and vendors anticipate lowering the price about 10 percent for buyers, but that's not always the case. Watch for sales tags, store policies, or prices marked "firm." That will give you a good idea whether there's some wiggle room. Stores and vendors sometimes require buyers to spend over a certain dollar amount or pay with cash or check to get a discount.

Shopping Yard Sales

Going out early on a Saturday morning to search for yard sales can be thrilling. You never know what you're going to find. You may come home empty-handed, or you may hit the mother lode. Will today be the day you find what you've been searching for? The thrill of this hunt is like no other.

Take cash. People selling stuff on their driveway are not going to accept credit cards or personal checks unless they know you well.

Start early. The best stuff is going to go early, so you need to hit as many as you can before about 10:00 a.m.

Go prepared. Go with an empty van/truck if you're looking for furniture. Be prepared to find what you're looking for and get it home.

Don't buy things just because they're cheap. I once found a vintage kidney-shaped desk for $1. It was a piece of furniture for a buck! How could I pass it up? Well, it was falling apart and needed extensive repair to make it usable. Be selective. Don't get swayed when you're out in the field.

Don't feel obligated to buy something. If there isn't anything you like, just say thanks, wish them a good sale, and be on your way. This may sound like a silly suggestion, but if you're a people-pleaser, you may find it tough to walk away from hopeful sellers who have been sitting in lawn chairs on their driveway all morning.

Dress down. It's true that some people will quote a higher price for people who look like they have money burning a hole in their pocket. A yard sale is not a place to pull a stack of twenties out of your designer purse or drive up in a limo. Dress comfortably, and don't give away too much about how much you have to spend.

Go often. Some days will be a wash; others will be amazing. You never know, but the more you're out there, the greater your chances are of snagging the next great find.

It never hurts to ask. If I come across a yard sale that has a lot of antiques, furniture, or home decor, I'll ask if there's anything else they want to get rid of. I've had people open their garage and let me have my pick of things they just didn't want to haul out or they thought wouldn't interest anyone. Nothing ventured, nothing gained.

Plan your route. Check a local paper to find sales you might be interested in, and map out an efficient path from one to the other. It's nice to have another adult with you so one can drive and the other can navigate and spot sales. (This also reduces the turning-on-a-dime-without-your-turn-signal-crazy-yard-sale driving that often happens.)

. . . .

Tip: Going to yard sales is a fun thing to do with your entire family. Grab some breakfast before, and go to a park afterward. Give younger children a few dollars to manage, and encourage them to practice addition and subtraction as they find things they want to buy. Older children can help plan the morning route, navigate, and keep an eye out for things on your wish list.

. . . .

Shopping Flea Markets and Antique Fairs

Whether these markets are a weekly event or only happen once a year, they can be packed full of great deals. Shopping these venues is a lot like shopping yard sales, so take cash, start early, go prepared, and dress comfortably. You may have to wade through the tube socks, used videos, and antiquated computer parts, but there are some great things to be found.

Negotiate the purchase price. Haggling is expected, and most vendors price their pieces a little higher to have some room to negotiate. Making an offer is acceptable, but make sure it's reasonable. Offering $5 for something priced at $25 is not reasonable. Maybe offer $20 or $22, and always be polite. Vendors are not likely to give you a discount if you insult them or point out flaws in their stuff. "This is a piece of rubbish. Now, can I buy it at a huge discount?" That doesn't really work. Being an antiques dealer myself, I have learned that it is hard work. I hunt for each piece, clean it, fix it up, price it, pack it, and put a lot of time into it before I put it up for sale. Keep all of that work in mind when you're asking a vendor for a discount.

Take cash. Most vendors don't accept credit cards and are hesitant to accept personal checks. If vendors do accept credit cards, they have to pay a fee on every purchase, so they are less likely to give discounts. Cash in hand gives you more bargaining power, and it's just easier for everyone.

Go prepared. Bring a cart or rolling tote to haul around your finds. That will save you multiple trips to the car and from carrying around awkward pieces all morning. Your arms will thank you! Also bring a tape measure and measurements of your spaces (if you're looking for specific pieces of furniture) and samples of fabric and paint chips. This preparation will help you be more confident in your purchases.

Shopping Thrift Stores

You would be surprised at how many name-brand pieces and antiques I have bought from thrift stores. I've purchased vintage alabaster fruit for a quarter a piece, English ironstone for a few dollars, and high-end furniture labels at deep discounts. I've even bought things that were new and still in the box. Some thrift stores are nicer than others and carry different types of inventory, so look around to find ones that regularly have the sort of thing you're looking for.

Prices are firm. For the most part, prices at thrift stores are firm, and it's generally frowned upon to try to negotiate. The proceeds go to charity, after all. Look for sales or shop when the store is packed to capacity. Stores are more likely to knock down a price when they need to make room.

Don't be afraid to dig. Some thrift stores are very neat and organized, but most of them require some amount of digging to find the deals. Be patient and visit thrift stores often since the inventory is constantly changing.

I love Mondays. Monday is a great day in most thrift stores. People drop off carloads after weekend yard sales or efforts to clean out a basement, attic, or garage.

They're onto us! I have just a word of warning about thrift stores. Most savvy owners have caught on to "people like us" and have bumped up the prices on vintage and antique furniture, even if it's in poor condition. This practice will vary from store to store, so if you see inflated prices, move on to a different store or visit a few times to see if the prices are reduced. The days of "All chairs are $10" seem to be coming to an end, but not everywhere.

Shopping Online Classifieds

I know there's a creepiness factor in going to a stranger's home to buy something. But the majority of transactions are between two very normal people who just want to buy something or get rid of something. It is an awesome resource for bargain shopping, so it's worth looking into.

Check often. It's like hitting a flea market when it first opens or digging through the cart at the thrift store, the one that holds the contents that were just priced and haven't hit the sales floor yet. You have to catch the best things right when they're posted, because they might not last long.

Ask for pictures. I really hate it when people don't post pictures on their listings, but it can sometimes be a good thing. I requested a picture of a "$30 buffet." I received the picture, and it was a solid wood, vintage French provincial buffet. It would've been gone if there had been a picture, but most people don't bother to ask.

Do your homework. Know what you're looking for. If you need a piece for a specific spot, make sure you take measurements and ask for them if they aren't provided in the post. Ask questions like these: "Are the legs sturdy?" "Are the drawers dovetailed?" "Is it solid wood?" "Is it from a nonsmoking home?" "Do the drawers work properly?" Don't be afraid to lose the piece. If you can't get these answers, just keep looking.

Know your key search terms. There are a lot of listings, so I narrow it down by using my favorite keyword searches: *French*, *dresser*, *chair*, *antique*, and *vintage*.

Be a good buyer. Craigslist doesn't have a place to leave feedback, but it's still a good idea to be a good buyer. If you ask questions of a seller, make sure you follow up whether you're interested or not. If you say you're going to buy something, buy it. When I e-mail someone about a piece, I always let that person know I buy from Craigslist all the time, and I always show up with cash in hand. People are more willing to negotiate, hold a piece for you, or sell to you again if you're nice to work with. I've even had people send me an e-mail when they are going to sell other pieces they think I might want to buy.

Don't buy what you don't want. When I went to buy my first French provincial dining set, I was very excited by the picture, but when I saw it in person, it was a different story. The furniture was described as "a set in mint condition." It wasn't a set, and it wasn't in mint condition. I felt stuck. I sighed, looked at my feet, and knew I needed to say something. I hated the chairs. I didn't want the chairs. "Can I just buy the table?" "Sure." So I just bought the table. Don't feel obligated to buy anything. Just say thanks and be on your way if you don't want it.

Be safe. You do need to keep your personal safety in mind when buying from people you don't know. I don't ever go to pick up furniture by myself. It's just not smart. Remember that you are going into a stranger's home with cash, so make sure someone is watching your back. If a situation feels sketchy, just back out. Even the greatest bargain is not worth risking your safety.

Shopping Auctions

A lot of people are intimidated by auctions, so they won't go. When I first attended an auction, I realized that I had missed out on the best-kept secret for buying antiques. This is *the* source. It's the place where all the dealers go to buy things for supercheap and then mark them up and sell them to you and me. Why not cut out the middleman and hit the auctions yourself? I know auctioneers can be hard to understand, and you may have to stand around for a couple of hours until they get to what you want, and you get butterflies in your tummy just thinking of raising your paddle, but I assure you it will all be worth it in the end. And you will be hooked.

Here are some tips when you're ready to bid:

Know in advance what the terms are. Some auction houses charge a fee to buyers on top of the purchase price; others don't. Some accept credit cards, and others don't. Just be very clear, and ask questions when you get your paddle.

Take the time to view the items prior to the auction. It's important to inspect everything and know what you want to bid on. Don't bid on something you can't check out, or you may regret it.

Don't raise your paddle at the first price the auctioneer calls out. If you do, everyone in the room will know you're new, and they'll give you the evil eye. If a chair is up for bid, the auctioneer might say, "Who will give me $30 for the chair? $20? $15? $5? A dollar bill?" If you want that chair, that's when your paddle should go up. You might be the only one in the room who wants

that chair, and you'll get it for $1. If you had raised your paddle right away, you would've paid $30.

Be prepared. When you bid on an item, it's yours right then and there. You have to hold it on your lap or on the chair next to you or in a pile at your feet. Most of the time you have to get that furniture in your vehicle that night, and there's not always someone on staff to help you. Just be ready.

Forget the auction myth. I'm talking about the myth that says if you twitch your eye, you will end up buying a $30,000 oil painting you can't afford and don't want. I

know that gag is on every sitcom ever made, but it doesn't happen in real life. You have to clearly raise your number or obviously nod your head to confirm a bid.

Don't get carried away. Auctions are designed for you to get caught up in the bidding and get carried away. It's high pressure. There's a roomful of people looking at you and at the people you're bidding against. You really want it, and so do they. How high will you go? "Just one more bid. . . . Okay, one more, and then I'm done. Okay, I won't break $100. . . . Maybe not $200. I am going to win this thing if it kills me!" It is so easy to get caught up in the excitement, so set limits and don't get too emotionally attached to something until the auctioneer says, "Sold!"

Use an absentee bid. If you can't make it there for the day of the sale, most auction houses will take bids in advance and bid for you. This is also a great way to remove yourself from the emotion of bidding live. The house will notify you after the sale if you won any of the items you bid on.

. . . .

Tip: Most auctions can last for hours and sometimes all day, so take some snacks and a bottle of water with you. Auctions are also more fun with a friend. The time passes faster when you have someone to talk to, and you can help each other carry larger purchases to your car.

. . . .

Buyer Beware

When shopping secondhand in any venue, here are some things to stay away from:

- Wood furniture that is wobbly or has poor repairs, chipping veneer, warped boards, or water damage.
- Chairs with wonky legs. Those are very difficult to repair (trust me on this one), so it's best to pass them up.
- Furniture made out of laminate, pressboard, particleboard, or other inferior materials.
- Upholstered furniture that smells like smoke or pets or has stiff foam that needs to be replaced.
- Linens that are not machine washable.
- Pieces that are beyond your ability to repair or reinvent.
- Dressers that need very specific and rare hardware (it could be expensive to replace).
- "Fad" antiques that are currently in high demand. Certain antiques wax and wane in popularity. Don't buy pieces at their peak. Give it some time, and the prices will come down again.
- Things that are impractical for your family, lifestyle, or space.

What to Watch For

- Furniture made of solid wood or wood veneer. Wood can be sanded, painted, refinished, glued, and repaired. It's also a sign of a well-built piece.
- Dovetailed drawers, box joints, and other signs of quality construction.
- Pieces with great lines. Colors, finishes, and fabric can all be changed, so look for pieces with good bones to give a nice place to start.
- Maker's marks. Whether it's ironstone, silver, flatware, or furniture, look for a maker's mark. It can give you an indication of value, age, rarity, and quality.
- Architectural elements. Shutters, doors, corbels, windows, and molding can be used in a variety of ways in home decor and can often be found for a steal. I once bought an entire truckload of one-hundred-plus-year-old doors for $25.
- Things that are unique, curious, quirky, or great conversation pieces. I personally love things like scales, typewriters, binoculars, alarm clocks, and fans. I'm not using them for their intended purpose any longer, but I just love how they look.
- Anything that catches your eye! Some of my favorites are hand-painted signs, European grain sacks, trophies, silver, linen tea towels, French furniture, mirrors, chunky gold frames, and ironstone.

Other Great Places to Watch for Bargains

- *Estate sales.* I've bought some nice things from estate sales, but they are hit or miss. The prices depend a lot on the agency running the sale. Look at listings prior to attending, and you'll have a good sense of whether it's worth your time.

- *Discount stores*. Ross, TJ Maxx, Marshalls, and Home Goods are wonderful places to find pillows, lamps, bedding, and accessories.
- *Consignment shops*. These are basically high-end thrift stores, except the store acts as a broker between the buyer and the seller. Because the store takes a percentage of the sale, the prices are generally higher, but you can still find nice pieces on a budget.
- *Online marketplaces*. Sites like eBay and Etsy are awesome resources for accessories, specialty hardware, and even furniture. Just make sure you ask plenty of questions so you know exactly what you're buying.

ONE MAN'S TRASH...

I find a thrill and great satisfaction in buying a special piece at a bargain that's just right for my home. I love pointing at my chandelier and declaring, "I paid $4 for that at a yard sale!" There is a certain pride that can be found in discovering potential. I almost relish the moments when someone scratches her head at a piece I'm super excited about. I assure her, "Just wait and see. This is going to be fabulous." I enjoy the fact that I see something she doesn't.

> *In the right hands, the ordinary can become extraordinary.*

When people see my home for the first time, they don't ever say, "Oh, I see you shop at yard sales." Instead they comment on a unique piece or how nice our home looks. I'm the one who blurts out that half the stuff in the room was free, and I bought *that* piece for only $10 at Goodwill, and I found *that* one at a yard sale for $30.

Now I have a few homework assignments for you. Don't worry. None of these are graded, and there are no due dates.

- Your first assignment is to look around your house and pick one thing that you've never been very fond of. Look at it not for what it is but what it can be. You can even take it a step further and see that potential through.

- Second, go out to a secondhand store, flea market, or yard sale and look closely at things. Imagine what a piece would look like if it were refinished or had a fresh coat of paint. Try to think of new ways to use a piece. Look at things not for what they are but what they can be.

- Third, examine a situation in your life. Maybe it's where you live, where you work, your current financial state, or a health issue. Maybe you're right where you are for a special reason. You could be in the perfect position to learn a valuable lesson about yourself or to help someone else through a difficult time. Look at the situation not for what it is but what it can be.

- Last, pick one or two people in your life whom you don't have very much hope for. Look for opportunities to encourage and build into them. Let them know there is always hope and potential for greatness in their lives, no matter how many mistakes they've made. Look at them for who they can be not who they are.

I've always loved the fact that God sees potential in each of us, no matter how big we've messed up or how broken we are. Isn't it awesome that we can take that example and do the same thing—not only in castoff furniture, but in others and even in ourselves? I'm incredibly thankful for potential. It means that in the right hands, the ordinary can become extraordinary. 🌿

from Shari's barn

Chapter 5

MAKING THINGS NEW

SEVERAL YEARS AGO, my dear friend Shari and her family bought a 1908 farmhouse with a barn, some outbuildings, and about twenty-five acres. It sounds like a dream, but the house was dilapidated, and the barns were packed to the brim with stuff. There were mice nests in the kitchen cabinets, about a dozen junk cars on the property, and almost no foundation under the front of the house. To say it was a fixer-upper would be a gross understatement. I spent most Saturdays at their farm, helping them with the overwhelming task of cleaning out the barn and outbuildings.

When I first looked in the enormous "long barn" filled at least waist-high with damp boxes, cat-urine-soaked couches, broken chairs, and mechanical parts, I thought, *Someone should just take a match to this place and call it done.* Upon closer inspection, though, I could see that some of the junk might not be junk at all, and it was worth taking time to sort through. It was dirty, tedious, and seemingly endless work, but it was rewarding as well. Not only were we cleaning up the mess, but we were also finding all sorts of things that were salvageable. Despite years of neglect, being exposed to animals, and enduring the changing climates, some treasures had survived.

Seeing forgotten castoffs being rescued and reborn made me look at "junk" in an entirely different way.

I remember a day when we uncovered a large steamer trunk under some boxes. Shari and I were both a little nervous about opening it. We were certain we would find a large family of insects or mice living in it. We opened the latch and flung back the lid. What we found was so surprising. In the middle of all of the junk and filth, inside this very sketchy-looking trunk, we found several white infant christening gowns, a pair of Victorian ladies' boots, a velvet riding outfit, a delicate beaded dress, and other articles of clothing and accessories. There were other days, though, when we opened a cabinet and found a mouse nest or made some other shriek-inducing discovery. And I certainly did my fair share of running off, slapping at myself, and squealing because I felt like something was crawling on me.

During the months (probably years) of cleaning out the barns and outbuildings, Shari and her family found furniture, artwork, leather suitcases, steamer trunks, oil lamps, tables and chairs, china, and antique farm equipment. A lot of what was discovered needed repair, refinishing, or a thorough cleaning at the very least, but it still had value—and some of it was very valuable. They used many of their finds to furnish and decorate their house. I already loved antiques, but this experience made me look at "junk" in an entirely different way.

It's now a common thing for me to bring home a neglected piece of furniture with missing drawers, stained upholstery, broken legs, or a marred finish. I can buy the piece for practically nothing because I see what the seller doesn't. It still has value. It's not beyond repair, and I can give it a new life and make it beautiful and useful.

NOT BEYOND REPAIR

About a year after starting my business, I started writing a DIY/home blog. At first, it was just about sharing my love of decorating; but as the blog grew, I began to feel that it was important to be an encouragement to my readers, and that feeling began to take on a life of its own. Somehow God planned on using my imperfect words to affect the lives of other people. *Ummm, God,* I found myself thinking, *let my blog just be about decorating. I've got my own issues. I'm not someone You want to use in this way.*

But when the feeling kept nagging at me, I would finally sit down and share on my blog what was on my heart. The response from my readers to posts like that was always overwhelming. Evidently, God *was* going to use me despite my protests, imperfections, and errors. In fact, I believe He uses me *because* of those. It doesn't matter how big I mess up, God never sees me as junk or hopeless. He always sees that I still have value. I am not beyond repair. He can give me a new life and make me beautiful and useful. And that's true of you too!

Just remember that it's not about perfection.

ARE YOU READY?

So, are you ready to look at things in a new way? To see value in that dated dresser your husband acquired as a bachelor or that hideous hutch you've had to tolerate because you really need the storage? Are you ready to give those pieces new life? All you need is an hour or two, some paint and supplies, and a few of my favorite furniture makeover tricks.

First of all, don't be intimidated if you haven't painted or refinished a thing in your life. The paints and techniques I am going to share with you are so forgiving that it's almost impossible to mess up. Just remember that it's not about perfection.

FURNITURE STRIPPING

The first three times I tried stripping a piece of furniture, I gave up halfway through and threw the piece in the trash. Yes, I did. It was messy and labor-intensive, and I hated every second of it. But the challenge of furniture stripping kept revisiting me. I would see beautiful pieces for sale, but I would pass them by because I knew they needed to be stripped. I just wasn't sure if I was ready to face that again.

A couple years later, I was at an antique store and found a table with gorgeous carved legs. (I'm a leg girl when it comes to furniture.) It was caked with layer upon layer of paint, and I knew it would need to be stripped. I loved it so much that I bought it anyway. Since my last paint-stripping endeavor, lots of water-based, nonstinky, easy-to-use products had entered the market. I purchased one of those and got ready to strip the piece. *The details in those legs are going to be the death of me*, I thought. So I decided to just strip and refinish the top and then paint the legs. That decision (which was a little lazy, I'll admit) established one of my signature looks—a refinished wood top on a painted base. Since then I've stripped dozens of table and dresser tops, and I've learned how to make it as painless and mess-free as possible.

Here's what you'll need:

- A piece of solid wood or wood-veneered furniture
- Water-based paint stripper
- Solvent-resistant gloves
- Eye protection
- Chip brush
- 3-inch putty knife
- Empty paint can
- Medium-grade steel wool
- Odorless mineral spirits

Step 1

Step 1: Apply Paint Stripper

While wearing gloves and eye protection, use a chip brush to apply paint stripper in a thick, even coat to top of table or dresser. Make sure to apply stripper to sides of top as well. Follow manufacturer's instructions, but I usually leave remover on for thirty to forty-five minutes or until I can see that the paint or finish is separating from the wood.

Step 2: Scrape Paint

Don the gloves and fashionable eyewear again. (Who doesn't look cute in oversized plastic glasses?) Then use the putty knife to scrape off the paint stripper. Keep gentle pressure on the putty knife; be careful not to gouge the wood surface. Put scrapings into empty metal paint can. Use edge of putty knife or a steel wool pad to get into details or curved edges. If paint or finish doesn't cleanly lift off with the first application, don't force it. Clean off what you can on the first pass and repeat the process as many times as necessary.

Step 2

Step 2

Step 3: Clean Surface

Pour a small amount of mineral spirits onto wood surface and scrub clean with a steel wool pad. This will clean off any remaining paint or finish as well as residue from the paint stripper. Scrub the surface until the raw wood is fully exposed and clean. Use a new steel wool pad if one gets gummed up. If a finish still remains on the wood, repeat steps 1 and 2; then clean the surface with mineral spirits again. Once wood is dry, it's ready to be sanded, stained, and waxed.

Some wood can be revived without fully refinishing. If the wood is pretty, but simply dried out or spotted from water damage, rub an oil and vinegar solution (3/4 cup oil to 1/4 cup vinegar) into the wood. Sometimes rubbing a wood stain similar in color to the original finish and protecting it with paste wax will also give the piece a new look without the mess. If the original finish is badly scratched or damaged or there is a thick polyurethane coat, the piece does need to be stripped and refinished.

The Power of Paint

Paint is one of my very favorite ways to give a tired piece of furniture a new look. I even like painting perfectly good pieces of furniture. (Gasp!) It customizes the piece and can bring out details that might otherwise go unnoticed. I know some people shudder at the thought of painting over wood, and I agree with them in certain cases. Extremely old pieces that are in mint condition or

Remember—it's just paint and can always be removed down the road.

have the original paint or finish would be devalued if painted. However, most run-of-the-mill antiques and vintage pieces that are dented and well used will not be ruined if painted. Remember—it's just paint and can always be removed down the road.

My only warning is that painting furniture can be addictive, so don't succumb to the temptation to paint every piece of furniture you own in the same color with the same finish. Mix a few painted pieces with wood pieces, and change the colors, shades, or value of the paint used so that it looks like the room was collected over time instead of completed in a twenty-four-hour makeover spree.

MILK PAINT AND CHALK PAINT

There are differences between milk paint and Chalk Paint, but I use them in almost identical ways. Milk paint generally comes in a powder form and has to be mixed with water just before use. It also can be unpredictable in how well it will adhere to a surface, but that's one of my favorite things about it. It will naturally flake away from certain finishes to give the piece an authentically aged look. If you want the paint to adhere, add a specialty bonding agent directly to the milk paint. It will then stick to old finishes, metal, and other slick surfaces. I prefer to use the paint without the bonding agent since I love the look of chippy paint.

Chalk Paint by Annie Sloan comes premixed by the quart. It has a thick consistency and great adhesive qualities, so it doesn't require priming, sanding, or other prep work prior to painting. It can be painted directly over factory

finishes, latex, oil paint, leather, metal, fabric, and even laminate. I rarely use latex paint on furniture since I discovered these two paints. It's certainly all right to use latex, but both milk paint and Chalk Paint distress beautifully and give a freshly painted piece a time-worn quality.

Milk Paint

What you'll need:

- Milk paint
- Warm water
- Plastic cup or container
- Stir stick
- Paintbrush (my favorite is a 2¹⁄₂-inch sash brush)
- Something to paint

Step 1: Mix Paint

I have found one brand of milk paint (General Finishes) that comes premixed in quarts, but most varieties come in powder form (Miss Mustard Seed's Milk Paint, Old Fashioned Milk Paint, and Homestead House). Mix roughly equal parts milk paint powder with warm water in a plastic cup or container. Paint colors can be mixed if you desire a custom color. Just make sure you mix enough for your project! (I have found that one cup of water and one cup of paint will be enough for a large dresser.) Stir paint with stir stick until paint is relatively smooth. Now, this is where some people get flustered with milk paint. There may be a few lumps left in the mix

or it may be too watery or too thick for your liking, but just keep working with it until it's what you want. I sometimes use a very watery mix, so the coat of paint is very thin and a lot of wood shows through. Other times I like a thick mix, so the end result has a lot of texture and an opaque finish. If you come across lumps when you're painting, just work them out with your brush.

. . . .

Tip: The texture of milk paint improves if it's allowed to sit for an hour or two before use. The powder absorbs more of the water, and there are fewer lumps.

. . . .

Step 2: Apply Paint

I prefer not to prime or sand prior to using milk paint so it will flake away and distress easily. Paint your piece of furniture using a brush (a foam roller can be used for larger surfaces). Keep your brush strokes long and even so that paint goes on smoothly. Once the first coat is dry, apply a second coat if needed. Allow paint to fully dry before distressing or waxing. As the milk paint dries, it may start to pull away from the surface, creating a crackled effect. A furniture wax or protective topcoat must be applied to milk paint to make it durable and water resistant.

Milk paint is perishable, so once mixed, it can only be stored for a couple of days. Put it in a lidded plastic, metal, or glass container and keep in a cool, dry place. I prefer to mix it in small batches to minimize the waste.

Chalk Paint

What you'll need:

- Chalk Paint
- Paintbrush
- Piece of furniture
- Fine-grit sanding sponge

Step 1: Apply Paint

Because prep work isn't required with Chalk Paint (hooray!), you can get right to the fun part—the painting. First remove

hardware and drawers from piece. Chalk Paint is best applied in one coat that is not overbrushed. The paint is thick and has a lot of texture to it, so apply it in long, smooth strokes. It also dries quickly, so don't brush over an area too many times or it will start to pull from the surface.

Chalk Paint thickens with age, so simply add some water and stir to thin.

Step 2: Smooth Paint

If you are not planning to distress the piece and want a smooth finish, use a fine-grit sanding sponge (the higher the number, the finer the grit) and lightly go over the flat surfaces once paint is fully dry. Stay away from corners, edges, and details so that you don't rub the paint off. Chalk Paint will sand off in a very fine powder,

so it's easy to create a supersmooth finish. When the finish is smooth to the touch, it needs to be sealed to protect it from water and wear, so skip over to "Waxing" for those instructions. If you want a distressed finish, skip this step of smoothing the paint. You're ready to try out some of my favorite distressing techniques.

. . . .

Tip: Wax can also be applied directly to Chalk Paint prior to distressing. It reduces the dusty mess and gives a different look. I prefer to distress prior to waxing, but you should try both methods to see which you prefer.

. . . .

DISTRESSING

Although I don't think every single piece of furniture needs to be distressed, I am a huge fan of distressed furniture. It brings out the lines of a piece and gives it character and a sense of age. And the process is so forgiving. It's especially ideal for a busy family with kids and pets. It doesn't matter if a piece gets scratched or dinged if it's already been intentionally roughed up. "It's okay if you drive your cars on Mommy's dresser, buddy. You're just adding to the aged look I'm going for."

I distress my furniture after the paint is dry and before I apply the wax. Distressing can be done after a piece is waxed, but then an additional coat of wax is required. Since distressing can kick up quite a bit of dust, make sure to wear a dust mask or respirator. (Come on. Who doesn't look cute in a dust mask? *With* oversized plastic glasses?)

When I'm distressing a piece, I try to give it a story. I imagine how it got into this condition. Was it from years of gentle use? Was the paint worn away over time or gouged and scratched off? Creating a story behind your work will make it look convincing and hard to tell from a piece that was distressed naturally over time. It is also important that the technique makes sense for the piece. Pieces with clean, modern lines or a traditional shape might not look good heavily distressed, scratched, or scraped. There are no set rules, so just go with your gut.

Lightly Worn

To create the look of paint that has worn away over time from gentle use, rub a fine-grit (100 to 220 grit) sanding sponge on just the edges and high points

of the piece. Also sand where wear naturally happens, like where your hands naturally rest on the arms of a chair or around the handle of a drawer or a hinge.

Scratched and Scraped

For a look that may have resulted from a piece being moved often or from years

of hard wear, use a medium to coarse sandpaper (50 or 60 grit). Press paper firmly against furniture piece and slide across surface to create rough scratches. Make sure you follow your "story" as you decide where to put the scratches. Then take a putty knife and scrape the edges and high points of the furniture piece to remove the paint in chips. Finish with a fine-grit sanding sponge to soften the look.

Heavily Distressed

At times I want to take distressing to an extreme to get a dramatic look. For this, I pull out the big guns . . . a power tool. I like to use an orbital palm sander with a medium-grit sanding pad on it. When working with an electric sander, you have to be careful not to sand in one place too long, or you will rub away the wood as well. Work the sander mostly along the edges and high points of the piece and wherever paint would naturally wear away. Step back from the piece frequently to get an overall view of how the distressing looks. Most orbital palm sanders leave swirly marks in the paint, a telltale sign that a palm sander was used. Go over those areas with a fine-grit sanding sponge to blend in those marks and soften the effect. This crucial last step makes the look authentic.

WAXES

After a few years of working with water- and oil-based polyurethane topcoats, I finally tried furniture wax and have never gone back. Apply paste wax and soft wax over paints or stains with a brush or soft cloth, and then buff to a soft shine. I love the hand-rubbed look and warm luster that wax gives a piece, so it is my favorite topcoat by far. Waxes also come in brown stain colors that can be used to darken and protect raw wood or to antique a painted piece. The finish that wax provides is durable and easy to revive if it gets scratched or loses its luster. I use it on all my furniture pieces, including my kitchen table, and it handles Play-Doh, stuck-on oatmeal, and yogurt finger paintings quite well.

Wax will deepen paint colors and give them dimension, but it will also slightly yellow whites. Just be aware that if you want your piece to be bright white, you should use a nonyellowing, water-based product (like Benwood Stays Clear Acrylic Polyurethane or Minwax Polycrylic).

Applying Wax

What you'll need:

- Wax brush or lint-free cloth (An old paintbrush with bushy bristles would work fine as well.)
- Clear soft furniture wax
- Clean cotton rag for buffing

Step 1: Apply Wax

Swirl brush or rag in wax, and then apply a thin coat to furniture. Work wax until it's absorbed into the paint or finish. If too much wax is applied, quickly spread it out with the brush or cloth.

Step 2: Buff

Allow wax to dry to a haze or until it's only slightly tacky to the touch. The drying time varies greatly depending on the type of wax, so read the manufacturer's instructions. I usually wait about fifteen minutes. Once the wax is dry, buff it with a soft, clean rag. Apply moderate pressure to the rag and rub in a circular motion, just like buffing a waxed car. Buffing pads are also available for orbital sanders, and a sander is great to use on large, flat surfaces like dining room tabletops. If you want a shinier finish, apply a second coat of wax—or more—until you're happy with the results.

Antiquing with Dark Wax

Dark wax is a great product for antiquing painted furniture, but it does take some practice to get a natural look that isn't streaky or overdone. Apply it directly to a painted surface to slightly stain the paint and make it appear darker. I like this technique for dark grays and reds that I want to tone down. But I usually use dark wax after a piece already has a coat of clear wax to keep the paint from being stained. This allows the dark wax to sit on top of the paint instead of penetrating it.

What you'll need:

- Wax brush (or bushy paintbrush)
- Clear soft furniture wax
- Dark furniture wax
- Clean cotton rag

Step 1: Apply Dark Wax

Dip your brush into the clear wax, and then dip just a corner of it into the dark wax. Brush the wax onto the piece of furniture, working the clear and dark wax together for a soft look. Brush away from the dark wax to spread it out and blend it. Repeat this process, remembering to tell a story about how the furniture was discolored. I like to antique in places that are commonly touched because oil from human hands will slightly darken a painted surface. Apply the dark wax around handles, edges of drawers, or where a cabinet door would be grasped.

. . . .

Tip: Use a grease-cutting detergent such as Dawn to shampoo paintbrushes after using them for wax. Work the soap deep into the brush, rinse, and then squeeze dry. Repeat this process until the water coming out of the brush is clear.

. . . .

Step 2: Buff

Allow wax to dry until slightly tacky to the touch. Then buff with a clean cotton rag.

A few more tips on working with waxes . . .

- Both milk paint and Chalk Paint can be mixed with clear wax to wash a color over a base coat of paint. (Imagine a soft French gray washed over a creamy white.)

- Wax is temperature sensitive and will melt if it gets too hot, so store it in a cool, dry place. If it does melt, just put it in a cooler place until it solidifies again. It'll still work great.

- Most waxes have a strong odor, so use a respirator mask or work in a well-ventilated area.

REFINISHING WOOD

To refinish a wood piece, all old finishes and paint must be removed. The surface should be clean and dry.

What you'll need:

- Orbital palm sander or fine-grit sandpaper
- Two clean cotton rags
- Wood stain
- Latex gloves

Step 1: Sand Surface

If wood was stripped of old finishes or paint, make sure surface is dry. Use an orbital sander with fine-grit sanding pad or sandpaper to smooth wood surface and prepare it for staining. Remove all dust with a clean cotton rag.

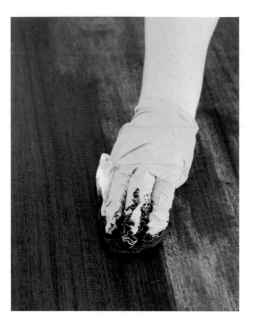

Step 2: Apply Stain

Wear gloves to protect your hands. Dip a corner of the rag into the stain until it is saturated. Apply to wood surface in long, smooth strokes with the direction of the wood grain. Repeat until entire surface is stained, being careful not to overlap areas that are already stained. If depth of stain color isn't achieved, a second coat of stain may be applied once first coat is dry to the touch.

Step 3: Finish

Once stain is fully dry, apply a coat of clear wax using waxing instructions on page 122. A liquid or spray polyurethane product may also be used if preferred. Apply multiple coats for additional protection and shine if desired.

·················

"CAN WE KEEP IT?"

I've shared my favorite techniques, but there are dozens of ways to paint, distress, and finish furniture. Finding your favorite combination of techniques and products will make your furniture unique. The entire process can be so much fun that you'll eagerly start looking for the next piece you can transform.

> *Once you start seeing potential in things and hone the skills to reveal that potential, it can be addictive.*

Now, don't blame me if your garage is soon so full of furniture to paint and refinish that you can't park your cars in there any longer. I don't want to get e-mails from upset spouses! Once you start seeing potential in things and hone the skills to reveal that potential, it can be addictive.

I've developed "lost-dog syndrome" for pieces of furniture. Jeff and I will drive by a yard sale, and I think he can feel the moment I spot a dresser I like. He knows that the "Can we keep it?" look is coming and that I'm about ready to ask him to turn around so we can go back for it. I can't help but rescue those little "puppies," clean them up, and find them nice new homes. I hope you enjoy making things new as much as I do. As you create your new treasures, I encourage you to find joy in the process and uncover not only the beauty in a piece of neglected furniture but also the gifts and talents you've been blessed with.

Chapter 6

CREATING A
HANDMADE HOME

YOU MAY HAVE FIGURED OUT that I'm pretty passionate about my home, and that passion can turn to crazy when it comes to some DIY projects. My floor-refinishing experience is only further proof. Most people, even seasoned DIYers, would probably call in a professional for something as big as refinishing the floors in four rooms and a hallway in their home, but not me. Some *smarter* DIYers who *were* going to tackle it themselves would do a lot of research or bring in a friend who had refinished floors before, but not me. I plowed ahead, confident in my ability to "wing it."

Before I proceed with this story, let me set the stage for you. It was early spring, so it was cold and rainy when I decided the project *had* to be done, which meant the windows could only be cracked, and drying time would be extended. Oh, and I was also five months pregnant with Calvin. Now, I don't think refinishing floors is normal "nesting"

I'm definitely a DIY optimist.

behavior, but I was done with having unfinished floors, and no one could talk me out of doing something about it. (Why couldn't I have just craved enchiladas and cheesecake like every other normal pregnant woman?)

I put on my respirator mask (a requirement, especially when pregnant) and got to work. I applied the dark walnut stain in thick, smooth strokes to get the deep color I wanted. It glistened and looked so rich and lovely. I was swelling with DIY pride . . . until it started to pool up, and I realized I had applied way too much stain and couldn't possibly walk across the floor to wipe it up. Maybe it would dry. I continued to the second room and hallway, certain it would all work out. (I'm definitely a DIY optimist.) I let the stain sit for a few hours and realized it would take months for it to dry in this cold, rainy weather. I had to come up with a different plan. I really needed some sort of rigging that would've been employed by a spy or a diamond thief, where I could be suspended about a foot above the floor and wipe up the stain without leaving a footprint. Not having one of those devices on hand, I had to think of something I could use to evenly disperse my weight. Could I stand on a piece of cardboard? In a cardboard box? With neither a rigging system nor a better idea, that's what I proceeded to do.

I stood (five months pregnant) in a diaper box and shuffled and hopped around the room, using an old towel to sop up the extra stain. Just to ensure that I looked thoroughly ridiculous, I had grocery bags over my hands in the absence of latex gloves. If this does not sound difficult (or ridiculous) to you, I would challenge you to try it. Then imagine doing it on a sticky floor with a decent-sized belly hanging out in front of you for about an hour. Per room. As I shuffled around in that diaper box, with my plastic grocery bag gloves and my respirator mask, I wanted to cry. My only thought was, *I hate this. I just want this to be over.*

THE REWARDS OF DOING IT YOURSELF

If you work on DIY projects long enough, you're going to end up with some good stories like mine. Despite my grumblings as I sopped up the stain, I learned a lot, not only about the *proper* way to apply stain (three rooms too late) but also about myself. I learned that my impatience can get me into trouble and that determination can get me through a frustrating project. It would've been so much easier for me to hire out the refinishing job, but if I had, I wouldn't have that story to laugh at and learn from. I also wouldn't have the reward of having done it myself, which I feel every time I see those rich, walnut-stained floors. I guess God made us with the desire to roll up our sleeves and dive into

> *If you work on DIY projects long enough, you're going to end up with some good stories like mine.*

work. In Proverbs 31, the virtuous woman is lifted as a model for burning the midnight oil and working hard. No wonder it's so fulfilling for us when we accomplish something ourselves.

That's not to say that every household improvement or project is a do-it-yourself job. We've paid professionals to do things that were beyond our skill, things like plumbing, electrical work, and more complicated upholstery. Hiring someone can at times make sense for your schedule, family, or project, but there's no denying that it's special when something was fashioned with your own two hands. It's the handmade touches that make your home entirely "you." My hope for you and myself as we're working through a long project list or even mundane household chores (yes, laundry too) is that we will find great satisfaction in the work, we will learn things that help us grow, and we will enjoy the process (or most of it!).

LET'S GET TO WORK!

Are you ready to get to work and make a few handmade items for your home? I hope my refinishing story didn't scare you off! Let's start with something super simple. If you can sew a straight line, you can make a pillow. We'll then get a little more advanced with a project that involves both building and slipcovering, but I'll break it down and hold your hand through it.

Faux Grain Sack Pillow Tutorial

I love the look of European grain sacks, but they can be pretty expensive. They are easy to make from scratch, though, using one of the most humble fabrics around—canvas drop cloth. The nubby texture of the fabric and loose weave are a thrifty alternative. Simple hand-painted detail completes the look.

What you'll need:

- Pillow form (I prefer feather filled)
- Small canvas drop cloth
- Clear quilting ruler
- Pencil
- Sharp scissors
- Cotton piping (enough to wrap around the perimeter of the pillow form)
- Sewing machine (equipped with a zipper foot)
- Coordinating all-purpose cotton thread
- Painter's tape
- 1/2-inch flat or angular shader brush
- Dark blue acrylic craft paint
- 1.0 artist liner brush
- Pins
- All-purpose sewing needle

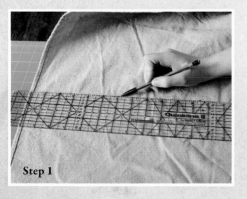

Step 1

Step 1: Measure and Cut Fabric

Wash drop cloth to soften. If the pillow form measures 18 by 18 inches, use a ruler and pencil to measure and mark two pieces of fabric to approximately 18 1/2 inches by 18 1/2 inches. The additional half inch is for a seam allowance.

Step 2: Make Trim

Cut piping to a length long enough to wrap around the perimeter of the pillow. Add about 2 inches to allow for some overlap where the ends meet. Cut a strip of drop cloth approximately 1 inch wide and long enough to cover the length of the cotton piping. If that length can't be achieved in one piece, sew two pieces together end-to-end. Fold strip of cloth over cotton piping and use a machine equipped with a zipper foot to sew tightly into place.

Step 2

Step 2

Step 3: Paint Fabric

Tape off desired number of stripes down the center of the fabric with painter's tape. With the blue acrylic paint and 1/2-inch flat brush, paint in the stripes.

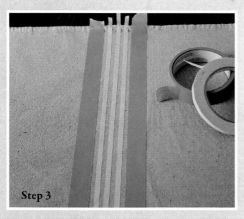

Step 3

Remove the tape immediately. Allow the paint on the stripes to dry. Lightly sketch initials on either side of the stripes. They can be as fancy or as plain as you'd like, or you can leave them out altogether. Paint the initials using the 1.0 liner brush, and allow the paint to dry. I used an antique grain sack as inspiration for my pillow.

Step 3

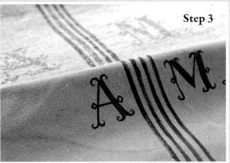
Step 3

• •

Tip: If you're uncomfortable painting freehand, find a font you like on the computer, size it for the project, and print it. Position the printed letter behind the fabric and hold both up to a window. The light from the sun will shine through the window, serving as a light box. Trace the lettering with a pencil and then paint. You can even embroider the stripes and monogram if you're better with a needle than a brush.

• •

Step 4: Assemble Pillow

Place the painted piece of fabric on your work surface with the right side facing up. Place the piece of drop cloth cut for the pillow back on top. Line up edges.

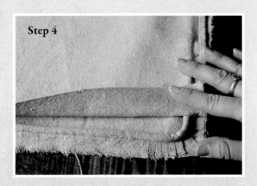
Step 4

Starting at the bottom of the pillow, pin trim into place around the perimeter of the pillow (pin through both layers of fabric). Make sure raw edges of fabric pieces and trim are facing in the same direction. Allow trim to overlap at bottom of the pillow.

Step 5

Step 5

Step 5: Sew Pillow

Still using a zipper foot on the machine, sew edges of the pillow cover together, pressing the foot tightly against the trim. Leave an approximately 8-inch opening at the bottom of the pillow to insert the pillow form. Remove pins and turn the pillow right-side out. Gently insert pillow form, and pin together fabric and piping to close the gap. Using a needle and thread, sew closed by hand with a basic running stitch. Trim all loose threads.

This simple pillow can be made with an unlimited array of fabrics and trims. Once you're comfortable with a basic pillow like this one, you can start getting fancier by adding button closures, zippers, and ribbon ties.

Ottoman Tutorial

Now that we've warmed up with some light sewing, we're going to go straight into a building project. Making an ottoman may sound like a daunting task, but we're going to keep this one simple. Simplicity doesn't mean plain, though. By using turned legs purchased from a hardware store and making a pleated slipcover for it, you can make your ottoman look like it's straight out of a fancy catalog, but you will have it at a fraction of the price.

For the slipcover, we're using a pin-fitting method, which means you'll assemble the slipcover in pieces using the ottoman as your dress form. Everything is done inside out, so make sure the raw edges are always facing out so they won't show when the slipcover is turned right-side out. I'll remind you along the way!

What you'll need:

- 3-by-3-foot piece of 3/4-inch-thick plywood or MDF (medium-density fiberboard)
- Tape measure
- One small nail
- Hammer
- 1 1/2-foot length of twine
- Pencil
- Eye protection
- Jigsaw
- Square
- Four turned, 9-inch wooden legs
- Drill and drill bits
- Eight 1 1/2-inch wood screws
- Dark walnut wood stain
- Clean rag
- Latex gloves
- Spray semigloss polyurethane
- Casters (optional)
- Two yards 4-inch-thick high-density foam
- Two yards 2-inch-thick foam
- Electric bread knife or serrated knife
- Two yards 1-inch-thick premium densified batting
- Spray adhesive
- High-loft quilt batting (twin-size)
- 3 yards of muslin
- Scissors
- Pins
- Staple gun and staples
- Sewing machine (with a zipper foot and heavy-duty needles)
- One 4-by-15-foot drop cloth
- Cream thread
- One 10-yard package of cotton piping
- Iron and ironing board

Step 1

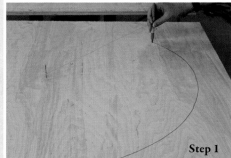

Step 1

Step 1: Cut Plywood Base

Step 1

Use your hammer to gently tap in a small nail at the center point of the plywood piece. Tie one end of the 1¹/₂-foot length of twine around the nail and one end around the pencil. Pull the twine tight, and trace a circle. Make sure to keep your pencil straight, so the circle is even. The circle should measure about 3 feet across. Remove the nail. Put on your protective glasses, and use the jigsaw to cut along the pencil line. Keep the saw blade just to the outside of the line. It's a good idea to have someone help you by holding the plywood steady as you cut it. Use two sawhorses, tables, or bar stools to rest the plywood on as it is being cut.

Step 2: Attach and Finish Legs

Working off the center point of the circle (marked by the nail hole), use a square to make a perfect X inside the circle. Using a drill equipped with a drill bit the size of the threaded screw on the turned leg, drill a hole for each leg at each of the four corners of the X. Thread legs in the holes. For additional stability, insert two 1^1/2-inch wood screws through top of the plywood into each leg.

Step 2

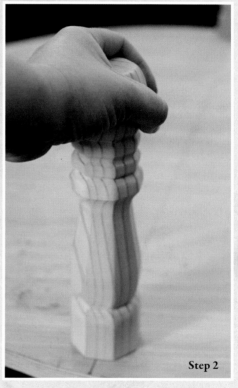

Step 2

With the plywood flipped over so the legs are facing up, use a clean rag to stain the turned legs. Wear latex or rubber gloves to protect your hands. Allow the stain to fully dry. Then spray with one coat of semigloss polyurethane. Allow poly to dry. If using casters, drill holes in the bottom of each leg, insert caster, and secure into place. (Because I'm using vintage casters, I used a dab of superglue to hold each caster in place.)

Step 3: Affix Foam and Batting

Use an electric bread knife or a long serrated knife to cut both layers of foam to the size of the plywood. It's tricky to get a clean, straight cut, but it's easier if you cut the foam larger than necessary and then trim the excess a little at a time. The edges will be covered by batting, so the cuts don't have to be perfect. Spray top of plywood base with adhesive, and stick 4-inch layer of foam into place. Spray the top of that foam layer with adhesive, and attach the 2-inch layer of foam.

Use sharp scissors to cut two pieces of 1-inch-thick premium densified batting to fit on top of foam. Then cut two pieces of high-loft quilt batting to fit on top of the foam. Spray some adhesive on the top layer of foam, and stick all three layers of batting into place. Apply a small amount of adhesive between each layer of batting to prevent shifting. Cut two pieces of batting to wrap around the sides of the plywood and foam. Spray the sides with adhesive and apply batting. Tip: Spray adhesive is very sticky, so work over a drop cloth to avoid a sticky floor. Trust me on that one!

Step 4: Make Muslin Cover

This muslin cover will be covered by a slipcover, so it doesn't have to be perfect. Cut a piece of muslin to cover the circular top of the ottoman, allowing

Step 4

about a 1/2-inch hangover as a seam allowance. Cut a second long piece of muslin to wrap around the side, leaving enough excess on the bottom to staple under the plywood base. If needed, sew two pieces of muslin together to use for the side. Wrap the

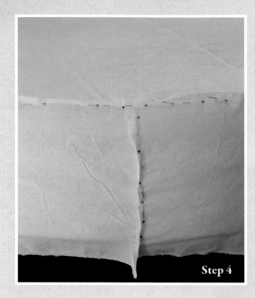

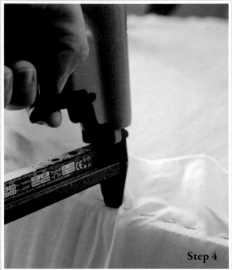

Step 4

Step 4

muslin piece around the side with the right side facing the ottoman. Pin ends together with the raw edges facing out. Remove from ottoman and sew seam. Return piece to ottoman, still turned inside out, and pin muslin top to the side piece. Remember to always keep your raw edges facing the same direction when you're pin-fitting. Once pinned, trim excess fabric (if there is any), remove from the ottoman again, and sew along the pin line. Remove pins. Turn muslin cover right-side out and gently fit onto ottoman. Turn the ottoman over and staple muslin cover into place. The muslin cover will prevent the foam and batting from shifting and pulling apart when the slipcover is removed for washing.

Step 5: Cut Slipcover Pieces and Make Trim

Prewash the drop cloth so that it's soft and can be washed in the future. Cut two 4-inch-by-15-foot strips from the drop cloth. Because the edges are already hemmed, these lengths will be used for the skirt. Set aside. Next, lay one end of the drop cloth over ottoman, and cut a circular piece of drop cloth to cover the top, allowing about 1/2-inch seam allowance. Cut a second long and narrow piece for the side of the ottoman that measures approximately 6 inches wide and is as long as the length of the remaining fabric (should be about 10 feet). With the remaining fabric, cover two lengths of cotton piping with drop cloth fabric. Each length should be approximately 2 inches longer than the circumference of the ottoman.

Step 5

(See page 138, Step 2 of the Faux Grain Sack Pillow tutorial, for details on making trim.)

Step 6: Assemble Slipcover

Wrap the side piece around the ottoman with the wrong side facing out. Pin tightly into place. Remove from ottoman, sew seam, and remove pins. Put side piece of fabric back on ottoman and pin top to side, sandwiching one length of piping trim between the two layers. Pin into place and allow piping ends to slightly overlap where they meet. Make sure the raw edges are all facing outward at this point. Remove from ottoman and sew layers together. Put slipcover back into place, still inside out. Fold up bottom edge and pin second length of piping along the edge, using the edge of the plywood as a guide to stay straight. Remove cover again and sew piping on. Remove pins. Turn slipcover right-side

Step 6

Step 6

out onto ottoman and test the fit. This is a good time to fix any mistakes. Don't worry if something's not perfect. Use a seam ripper to remove the mistake, and try it again. You're working with drop cloth, which is very cheap, so it's okay if you mess up.

Step 7: Attach Skirt

Sew both pieces cut for the skirt in Step 5 together end-to-end. Make sure hemmed edges of drop cloth fabric are on the same side, facing the same direction. Turn slipcover inside out and put on ottoman again. Start pinning skirt to bottom of cover, remembering to turn the raw edges out and have the hem pointing down.

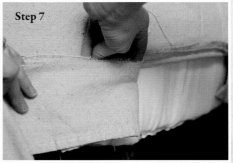

Pleat the skirt by folding it back over every 5 to 6 inches. Continue around the entire skirt, pinning as you go. Where the ends of the skirt meet, pin the two pieces together with the raw edges facing out. Trim excess fabric if there is any. Sew where the skirt ends meet first, and then sew the skirt onto the cover. Remove pins and trim stray threads. Turn the slipcover right-side out and iron the pleats.

YOU NEVER KNOW UNTIL YOU TRY . . .

If you're intimidated by the thought of making things from scratch, don't be! I know some of the projects in this book, especially the ottoman, may look complicated, but they're not. Remember that a mountain isn't climbed in one big leap. It takes many smaller steps to reach the top. Just take these projects one step at a time.

You do not have to be a "crafty" person to create a handmade home.

You also have to remember that on my blog and in this book, I'm sharing things I've made after years of practicing and refining my skills—and I'm still refining them. The truth is, I've made a lot of things along the way that were downright awful. I've had my share of epic failures as I learned how to sew, build things, and make things from scratch. Lots of projects have ended up in a Dumpster because I couldn't stomach looking at them any longer. I've learned I'm far too impatient for quilting, crocheting, and knitting. After making throws and wall hangings that were warped, bubbled, crooked, and far from fine craftsmanship, I packed away my skeins, hooks, and needles and tried other projects that I might have a knack for.

You also do not have to be a "crafty" person to create a handmade home. Woodworking, sewing, and painting are all learned skills, not ones we're blessed with at birth. When people come into my home, they'll often say things like, "I love what you've done, but I don't know how to paint." I didn't either until I picked up a brush and gave it a try. All of us have doubts that prevent us from trying new things and stepping out of our comfort zones. Too often the fear of failure rears its ugly head.

I'm working through this currently with my son Marshall. He's at the perfect age to learn how to ride a two-wheel bike, but he's scared of falling. His fear is so strong that he doesn't even want to try. As his parents, Jeff and I can see the day when Marshall is eight or ten years old and other neighborhood kids are riding their bikes to go get ice cream. If he doesn't know how, he'll miss out on something he would enjoy. But he can't see that right now. Do you resist trying new things for fear of falling?

If you're just sitting around wishing and hoping you could paint, sew, or build things, set aside that fear of failure, the doubts, and those voices that tell you you're not crafty, creative, or skilled enough. Remember that everyone starts somewhere, and be patient with yourself as you hone your abilities. Don't allow a fear of falling to let you miss out on all the things you might enjoy. Yes, you might fall. You might fail spectacularly. (DIY projects are often accompanied by tears, setbacks, and sometimes even scooting around in a diaper box!) You might discover you hate sewing and have zero patience for it. Or you just might discover a hidden talent. Painting might become your new favorite hobby! God might have blessed you with the ability to make the most amazing slipcovers, and soon you'll have friends asking you to make some for them. You just never know until you try. So try. Find satisfaction in the work, grow through the lessons learned, and enjoy the rewards of doing it yourself.

Chapter 7

DECORATING
DOLLARS AND SENSE

W HEN FLIPPING THROUGH decorating magazines, I sometimes come across a $2,000 side table or a $700 lamp that is
labeled as a great bargain. I'm assuming there must be a voucher
for my son to attend the college of his choice in one of the side-table drawers or
sewn into the shade of that lamp. Now, *that* would be a bargain! Some people may
think those pieces are a deal even without the college voucher, but I'm not one of
those people. I'm guessing you're not either. Although I confess that at times I
wish I had an unlimited decorating budget, I do really love the fact that my home

has been created on a small budget. After all, money can't buy love or happiness, and it's not totally necessary to create a beautiful home either.

I once added up the total cost of my living room, which has been featured in a magazine, and we had only spent $758 from floor to ceiling over about four years. One of my favorite pieces, the one-hundred-year-old piano, was totally free. We had just moved to Pennsylvania and were still in the early stages of furnishing and improving our home. Our church held a yard sale, and when I went to peruse the bargains, I was so excited to see a picture of a beautiful antique piano for sale. I grew up in a very musical family, and I had wanted a piano in our home for years. We finally had the space. Maybe we could get one. I started to plan out where we would put it, but then I saw the price, and my heart sank. It was $300. There was no way we could afford it. I continued with my shopping and never mentioned it to Jeff.

A few days later, Jeff called me from work and told me he was going to be home late. I didn't think anything of it and went about my day. When I finally did hear the front door open, Jeff came into the family room and asked me to stay in the back of the house. "Ummm . . . okay." I sat in the family room rocking Marshall while I heard voices and grunting and furniture scooting on the floor. *What is Jeff up to?* I wondered. I had no clue. After about thirty minutes, Jeff invited me to come into the living room. There against the wall was *the piano*, the one I had fallen in love with at the yard sale.

"How did you get it? How did you know I wanted it?" I asked. My husband explained that the piano hadn't sold at the yard sale, so the owner asked the

> *Money can't buy love or happiness, and it's not totally necessary to create a beautiful home either.*

Almost anyone can create an amazing space with a limitless budget, but it takes a lot of creativity, resourcefulness, and patience to put together a space with limited funds.

church secretary if she knew anyone who might want it for free. Jeff was standing there when the conversation took place, and he claimed it for me. He knew me well enough to know that I don't care about chocolates and flowers, but a free antique piano will make me cry. (It's okay to let out a collective "Awww." It was very sweet of him.)

I could tell dozens of stories about beautiful things people have given us for free. And I could tell even more stories about amazing bargains I've come across and how I've been able to create the rooms in our home without breaking the bank. Putting together a room for as little as possible is not only a fun game of sorts, but it's also using good sense to make the most of the money and resources God has blessed you with. Almost anyone can create an amazing space with a limitless budget, but it takes a lot of creativity, resourcefulness, and patience to put together a space with limited funds.

To give you some ideas of how to stretch the decorating dollars in your decor, I'd like to highlight some of the freebies and great bargains on display in my own home. Cheap and chic can coexist, and you can put that to the test by implementing some of these ideas in *your* home.

LIVING ROOM

Best Bargain

When I was looking for drapery fabric, I fell in love with Waverly's Tucker Resist Chambray fabric, but the linen home decor fabric was way out of my budget at around $38 per yard. I found the exact same pattern in Waverly's Sun N Shade line for around $10 per yard. The pattern was printed on canvas and then treated to resist fading and moisture, which sounded perfect for curtains. I saved hundreds of dollars and still got the exact look I wanted.

Secondhand Finds

The living room holds several of my favorite finds. The bead board door over the piano was $2, the pair of side tables was $10, the Trumeau mirror was $25, the piano bench cost $5, and the coffee table was $35. Both the chairs benefited from new covers. The French chair was $25 (reupholstered in a drop cloth), and the wing chair (see page 157) was $65 (reupholstered with two antique European grain sacks, which cost $70 for the two).

Freebies

For this room, freebies included the curio cabinet, the sofa (which I slipcovered in a drop cloth), and the one-hundred-year-old piano.

Where I Splurged

One of my blog readers, who is a very talented artist, graciously offered to paint a cow for me after I expressed a desire to have one hanging in my home in a blog post. The original oil painting of the cow (whom I have affectionately named Eulalie) cost me just $150 for shipping.

DINING ROOM

Best Bargain

I have two in this room. The antique chandelier was $4 at a yard sale. It was dismantled and in a box, so others didn't realize what it was. I bought it hoping that all of the pieces were still there, and they were. Every single crystal. My

Detail of the typography on the "tattoo" bamboo mat in my dining room.

father-in-law rewired it for me, and I made the cord cover out of remnant curtain fabric. (Lesson learned—look in boxes at yard sales!)

I purchased the bamboo mat from a friend for $75. For a 6-by-10-foot rug that makes a huge impact in the room, that is a steal.

Secondhand Finds

I purchased the dining set for $300 but then refinished and sold the buffet for $250, making the cost of the table and six chairs $50. The antique doors were $40 for the pair.

Freebies

The corner cabinets, buffet, and high chair were all welcomed freebies.

· ·

Tip: If you can't afford a rug for your dining room, try painting one directly on the floor or on oil cloth. A sampler-style rug like the one in my dining room is easier to replicate than a more traditional design. You'll get the visual impact of a rug for just a few dollars of paint.

· ·

GUEST ROOM

Best Bargain

The exposed board wall has to be the best bargain in the room. I made it using two pieces of hardboard cut into planks and then nailed to the wall. It created a charming cottage look for under $30.

Secondhand Finds

Several pieces give this room a lot of character for very little money. The stool, the plant stand/side table, and the antique doors were each only $5. The dresser was $35, the French chair was $75, the lacework over the bed was $25, and the aqua table cost me $25.

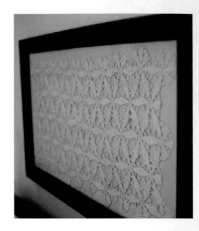

Freebies

The bed itself was free, as well as the antique equestrian prints. And I'm proud to display the antique coverlet made by my grandmother (heirlooms are often the best kind of freebies).

FAMILY ROOM

Best Bargain

I bought the pair of French armchairs at a yard sale for $10 each, and they didn't even need a makeover! (My mom disagrees with that, but I love them just as they are.)

Secondhand Finds

The tobacco basket, desk chair, and French side chairs were each $25. The coffee table cost me only $18.

Freebies

No-cost, big-impact finds include the daybed, desk, and wing chair (slipcovered in drop-cloth fabric).

Splurges

This big room required a few splurges, although they were still great deals. The antique stepback cupboard was $225, the buffet/TV console was $300, and the dresser was $125. And $99 was a reasonable price for the whimsy and charm of the antique rocking horse.

MASTER BEDROOM

Best Bargain

My French dresser was purchased off Craigslist for $35. I did have to replace the hardware, which cost me another $70, but it's a very high-quality dresser that provides loads of storage. The sellers even contacted me when they were ready to sell the matching highboy.

Secondhand Finds

The side tables were $35 each, the French chair was $75, the highboy dresser was $65, and the shutters were $45 for the pair.

Freebies

Most people wouldn't guess that my lamps made out of antique columns didn't cost me a cent, and neither did the vanity or the vintage mattelasse bedspread.

. . . .

Tip: A lot of pieces I got for free were traded for my services, another piece of furniture, or advertising on my blog. Bartering is a great way to use what you have to get what you want.

. . . .

Maybe you're looking over my bargains and thinking, *People have never given me stuff that cool for free* or *My luck isn't that good at yard sales.* I know how you feel. When I see awesome makeovers for nothing, I usually feel that way too. Your time will come. Be persistent and patient, and you'll build a room you love at a price you can afford.

KEYS TO DECORATING ON A TIGHT BUDGET

Balancing the tightrope of chic and cheap is somewhat of an art form, but you can do it successfully by following some of these guidelines.

Flexibility—You can stay true to your style and vision and still be flexible. When your decorating funds are limited, you have to be an opportunist. Maybe you find a piece of furniture that's the perfect size, but the style is a little off. Perhaps painting it, replacing the hardware, or styling it in a particular way will make it fit your taste. You'll have a lot more options by being flexible.

> *When your decorating funds are limited, you have to be an opportunist.*

Patience—It does take time to put together a space on a shoestring, and the end result will be much better if you wait for what you want at the right price. If you rush into buying things that are the right price but aren't what you want at all, you'll probably regret it and want to spend even more money to replace it down the road. (I have done that more times than I'll admit in this book.) On the flip side, it's not a good idea to rush into buying something you love that is way over your budget. You may have the instant high that comes with finding what you want, but you may regret it later when the credit card bill arrives. Imagine how sweet it will be when you find what you want at a great price (or even free!). Just keep your sights on *that day* and practice patience.

Elbow Grease—You have to be willing to roll up your sleeves and do most (or all) of the work yourself when you're trying to make every cent count.

Get the Word Out—This may sound like odd advice, but this is how I've gotten so many things for very cheap or free. Just let people know what you're looking for, what you like, and what you need. I'm not suggesting you hand out a wish list to all of your friends, family, neighbors, and acquaintances, but don't feel shy about mentioning that you're working on your house and looking for a few key pieces.

DON'T BE JEALOUS—BE INSPIRED

When you do look through those high-end decorating books and magazines or find yourself drooling over a million-dollar home, don't assume that look is totally out of your reach. There is a lot of inspiration to take away from expensive rooms.

Color—Great color combinations are available on any budget. If you see a high-end room you love, figure out how you can use those colors in your own home. Certain websites and apps can even calculate the exact paint colors used in a photo so there's no guesswork involved.

Texture—Look at what textural contrasts are used in the space. Are warm woods mixing with sleek metallics? Or perhaps rough, natural textures are mingling with luxurious fabrics. Again, interesting textural contrasts can be achieved inexpensively.

Furniture Placement—Arranging the larger pieces well is a foundation to creating a great room. Try to find rooms in magazines that are a similar size and floor plan as yours, and then notice how the furniture is placed. Using a picture as a "map" can give you a good sense of the kind of pieces you should look for when on the hunt.

SECRET WEAPONS

The two secret weapons I use to get the most out of my home decor budget are paint and fabric. Those two things are the cheapest and most impactful ways to make over a single piece of furniture, a room, or an entire house. I would go so far as to say that even the most depressing, neglected space can be improved with paint and fabric. Do you need some ideas?

Paint

- Obviously, you can paint walls to make a room feel warm and cozy, open and airy, or bright and cheerful. Use all-over stencils to create the look of wallpaper at a fraction of the cost.

- Don't forget to paint the ceilings. A bright white matte ceiling, one in a soft sky blue, or even a stenciled ceiling can add a lot to a space. At the very least, paint will prevent a grimy-looking ceiling from detracting from the rest of the space.

- Woodwork, trim, and doors are other places to put paint to good use. Bright white trim can set off a soft wall color; a colored trim can frame out a room. Builder-grade doors become custom when they are painted an interesting color.

- Give yourself a new kitchen by painting the cabinets. Go with classic white, sophisticated black, or a pop of color with cherry red or apple green.

- With all the quality paint products available now, you can paint all sorts of unexpected surfaces—laminate counters, furniture, tile, metal, plastic, appliances, bathtubs, brick, and stone.

Fabric

- Use fabric in simple ways by making drapes and custom pillow covers. Lots of no-sew tricks can make these projects simpler. Use fusible webbing or fabric glue to hem the edges and the bottom of curtains as an alternative to "the machine."

- Fabric can be applied like wallpaper by using liquid starch. It will stay in place for years and can be removed by simply wetting the fabric with water. The fabric can even be washed and reapplied to the wall or used for a different purpose.

- Upholster furniture with inexpensive fabrics like drop cloth fabric, cotton twill, duck, denim, or canvas.

- Reuse old sweaters, tweed jackets, and stylish prints to upholster seat chairs, make a pillow cover, or even create Christmas stockings. Tea towels, tablecloths, coverlet spreads, and grain sacks can also be used as fabric for sewing and upholstery projects.

- Stretch a pretty fabric or vintage textile around a wood frame to create instant art.

- Use fabric to hide unsightly things such as laundry areas, open storage, access panels, or pipes under a kitchen or bathroom sink.

- Drape fabric behind and over a bed to create an instant canopy. You can also use fabric to create an upholstered headboard that's comfortable and stylish.

Tufted Upholstered Headboard Tutorial

This style of headboard sells for big bucks in fancy catalogs, but you can make it from scratch at a fraction of the cost. Tufting gives the headboard a classic, elegant look, and no one will ever guess it was a DIY project. Customize the size of the headboard to fit your bed. Make the headboard tall for a more dramatic look, or use a long and narrow version to create a daybed.

What you'll need:

- 3/4-inch-thick plywood or MDF cut to desired size and shape
- Jigsaw
- Eye protection
- Pencil
- Tape measure
- Drill equipped with drill and driver bits
- Spray adhesive
- Electric carving knife
- 2-inch-thick high-density foam, large enough to cover plywood
- 1-inch-thick premium densified batting, large enough to wrap around plywood and foam
- Scissors
- Fabric, enough to cover headboard and buttons
- Fabric button-covering kit
- 1/16-inch polyester cording
- Large upholstery needle
- Washers (at least 3/4-inch diameter, one for each tuft)
- Staple gun
- Staples
- Two 1-by-2-by-3-inch boards (optional)
- Table saw (optional)
- Stud finder (optional)
- Level (optional)
- 1 1/2-inch wood screws

Step 1: Cut Headboard Shape

For a simple, more tailored look, cut the piece of plywood into a rectangle. It should be 3 or 4 inches wider than the mattress and high enough to show above a propped bed pillow. (Mine is 26 by 64 inches for a standard queen-size bed.) To make a curved headboard, draw a curved design on one half of the plywood. Cut out the design with a jigsaw. Then flip the cut piece over to use as a template

Step 1

Step 1

for the other side. Trace with a pencil and cut out with a jigsaw. Make sure to wear protective glasses while using power tools. Tip: I bent a long plastic zip tie into the shape I wanted to create a line for the curve.

Step 2: Create Tufting Pattern

Using a tape measure or yardstick, determine the spacing for your tufts on the piece of plywood. I situated mine in a diamond pattern 6 inches apart. It is a good idea to start in the center and work your way out. Drill a 1/4-inch hole at each tuft to pull the needle through.

Step 2

Step 2

Step 3: Cut Foam, Batting, and Fabric

Spray plywood base with adhesive, and press 2-inch foam to surface. Because foam comes in 24-inch-wide pieces, it may be necessary to use more than one piece, depending on the size of your headboard. Once foam is in place, use an electric carving knife to cut foam to the shape of the headboard. Use scissors to cut the 1-inch batting several inches larger than the headboard. Leave enough overhang to wrap batting around the sides to later be stapled to the back. Stick into place with spray adhesive.

Step 4: Cover Buttons

Step 4

Following the instructions on the button-covering kit, cover enough buttons to tuft the headboard. The number of buttons you'll need depends on the size of the headboard and how full you want the tufting to look. I used thirty-nine on my headboard.

Step 5: Tuft the Headboard

Place fabric over batting on headboard, making sure fabric is centered and there is a generous overhang on all sides. Thread a 12-inch length of polyester cording onto upholstery needle. Start at the center tuft and push needle through the back of the plywood, all the way through the foam, batting, and fabric. Thread button onto needle. Insert

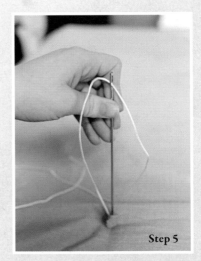

Step 5

177

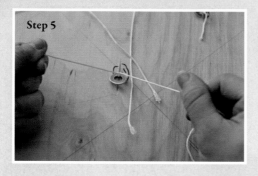

Step 5

needle back through the foam and the plywood hole. Pull both ends of polyester cording tight. This is a good time to enlist the help of a friend who can push the button in while you pull the cording tight. Secure the cording to a washer. Continue this process with all of the other tufts, working your way from the center out.

Step 6: Staple Fabric

Step 6

Wrap excess fabric tightly around the headboard and staple into place. Create tight folds in the fabric when necessary.

Step 7: Install Headboard

We installed our headboard on the wall using a locking cleat. Cut two 1-by-2-inch pieces of wood to a length of 3 feet. Rip (or cut lengthwise using a tablesaw) both pieces to a 45-degree bevel on one side. The two beveled sides will then fit together like a puzzle. Install one of the boards to the back of the headboard using $1^{1}/_{2}$-inch wood screws. Use a measuring tape to make sure the cleat is level and centered. The bevel of the cleat should be pointing down, with the short side against the headboard. Hold the headboard against the wall to determine where the second cleat should be hung. Mark the spot with a pencil, and use a level to mark a guideline for mounting the cleat. Use a stud finder to locate two wall studs; mark these spots with a pencil. Line up the cleat with the guideline, with the bevel faceup and the short end against the wall. Drill two

Step 7

pilot holes through the cleat and into each stud. Secure cleat in place with 1¹/2-inch screws. The headboard cleat will now fit into and hang from the wall cleat. Tip: When inserting the screws, make sure they are positioned so they don't protrude through the bevel and interfere with how the two halves fit together.

As an alternative to using cleats, you could attach rough legs to the back of the plywood, screw those into the wall, and attach them to the bed frame. Or simply use the legs to prop up the headboard and lean it against the wall.

. . . .

Tip: The foam is the most expensive part of this project, but costs can be cut by sandwiching a couple of layers of egg-crate foam (with the smooth side facing out) and topping it off with an old comforter instead of batting.

. . . .

PRACTICE MULTIPLICATION

God has blessed each of us with talents, relationships, and possessions, and we can find new ways to multiply all we've been blessed with, no matter how much or how little that is. When it comes to decorating, try multiplying your decor by selling some furniture and accessories you don't like at a yard sale or through Craigslist. Then use the money to buy things you do love and will use. When you do, shop smart and wait for the perfect piece at the perfect price. Or find a friend to barter with. If your friend loves to sew and you love to paint, offer to trade services. You'll both benefit.

Find new ways to multiply all you have been blessed with, no matter how much or how little that is.

Whatever your decorating budget is, you can create a gorgeous, comfortable home for your family. I hope you're looking around your house right now, imagining how you can use what you already have to entirely transform your space. And I hope you've been inspired to patiently work on your home as your budget allows. There are so many creative ways to put your decorating dollars and sense to good use. Once you've mastered the art of thrifty decor, you won't ever take a $2,000 side table seriously again. 🌹

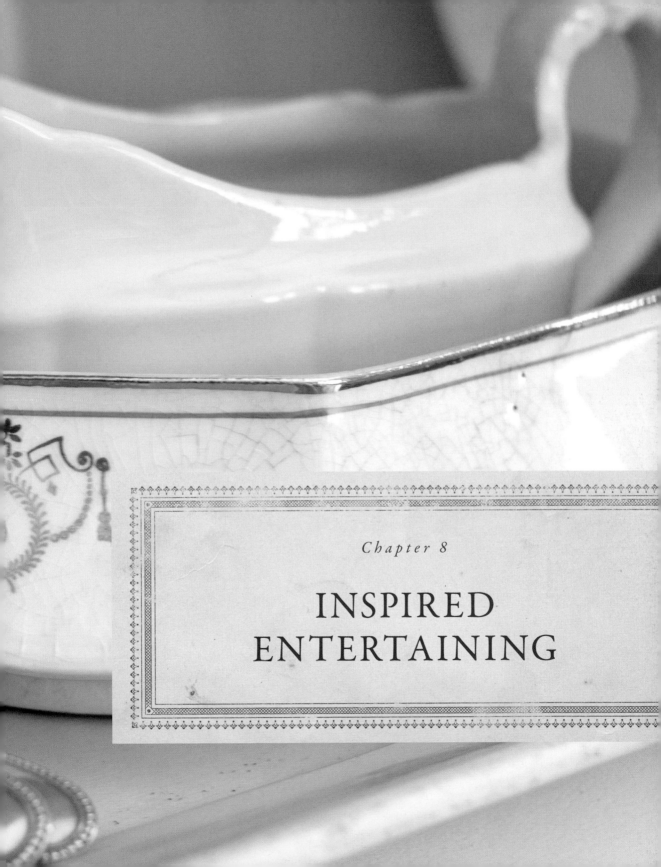

Chapter 8

INSPIRED
ENTERTAINING

I USED TO HAVE A LITTLE CHALKBOARD in my guest room. When I first hung it on the wall, I ran a search on the Internet for quotes about hospitality. Almost all of them were something horrible, like "Houseguests are like fish, they start to stink after two days" or "Hospitality is making your guests feel at home and wishing they were there." Well, those quotes weren't going on the chalkboard! Yes, it's nice to get your house back to normal after having guests, but hospitality shouldn't be something you have to try to get through like a root canal or refinishing your floors when you're five months pregnant (see chapter 6). Showing hospitality is an honor and one that can bring great joy to both the giver and receiver.

The most powerful example of hospitality I've experienced happened in my own home. We were moving into our house just outside Gettysburg, Pennsylvania. Jeff had been the youth pastor at our new church for only a few weeks, so we didn't know many people there yet. When moving day started, there were about four or five people who showed up to help us move in. We had a lot of stuff but little help, so I figured it was going to be a long day. My pregnant belly (I was about six months along) and I were posted at the front door to direct traffic. After the familiar volunteers made a few trips into the house, I started to see new faces. A pair of eyes would peek over a box, and the newcomer would ask, "Where's the staircase?" or "Where should I put this box?" I would direct each one to the proper room only to turn around and see another new face with an armload of stuff. I became convinced that the entire population of the town was there to help with our move, and I was ready to hug them all (it was probably the hormones).

During a lull in the traffic, I went to the kitchen to see how my mom was coming along with unpacking the food and dishes. The room was a bustle of activity and filled with an army of women. They were plugging in slow cookers, filling my refrigerator with casseroles and my pantry with baked goods, unpacking my dishes, and washing out the cabinets and drawers. Other people were out back, filling coolers with drinks for the volunteers. I was stunned and

> *You can have the most delectable spread of culinary creations, but if you don't have love for your guests, the food doesn't mean very much.*

overwhelmed. I'm sure I hugged several sweet ladies who were total strangers. The church even sent a beautiful bouquet of flowers to welcome us into our new home.

That was hospitality. These were people going above and beyond to make us feel welcomed, loved, and at home. They barely knew us—and some didn't know us at all—yet they were giving their time and their food to say "Welcome" with their actions. They were showing us love by so generously meeting our immediate physical needs and actually going well beyond.

That can be our goal every time you or I have guests in our homes—to not only meet their immediate physical needs of a drink, a meal, or a bed but also to make sure they feel welcomed, loved, and at home. Simple, heartfelt hospitality. You can have the most beautifully decorated table and the most delectable spread of culinary creations, but if you don't have love for your guests, the decor and food don't mean very much. On the flip side, you can have paper cups and plates on a card table, and if you pour out love on those you're with, it will be a memorable and meaningful time for all.

THE HOSPITABLE HOME

There was a time when a woman might have fainted if a dinner guest used the wrong fork for the wrong course. We have certainly lightened up! In this day and age, we can set an entire table with sporks and plowls (or is it blates?) that can be wrapped up in a plastic tablecloth that converts into an eco-friendly trash bag that self-destructs. (We may not want to take things quite that far, though.) Thankfully, I have some foolproof ideas for setting a lovely table or buffet without all the fuss.

It's Okay to Be Super Casual

I give you my full blessing and permission to use paper products when enter-taining. (I think we all do that anyway, right?) I totally understand that you want to have fun at your get-together instead of counting all the plates, glasses, and flatware that you will have to wash once everyone goes home. Pick out plates, cups, and cutlery that fit the occasion. Colorful and festive ones can be used for holidays, birthdays, and other celebrations. White or clear can look elegant for luncheons, teas, or showers.

It's Okay to Be Fancy Schmancy

I love setting a formal table and getting to use linen napkins, my mother's china, and my grandmother's silver flatware. If you love that sort of thing too, go for it! Just make sure it's still welcoming and the decor isn't the focus of the occasion. Formal tables can make people feel uncomfortable, underdressed, or uneducated about etiquette. Let people know you love setting a pretty table, but encourage them to relax. Assure them they can use whichever fork they want, and no one will faint if they choose the wrong one.

Mix and Match

For the best of both worlds, mix the casual with the formal. Sterling silver flatware can hang out with clear plastic plates, and a fancy creamer can hold plastic forks. Sometimes the juxtaposition of the pretty and the plain can look even better than pulling out all the stops.

. . . .

Tip: Cloth napkins can actually seem casual or formal, depending on how they are used. Tied with twine, they work well for a garden get-together, but beaded napkin rings will dress them up for a special event. I love the look of linen napkins, and I don't mind the ironing every now and then, but I totally understand when people have an aversion to the ironing board. If that describes you, lovely permanent-press napkins offer the elegance of cloth napkins without the starch and the iron. You can even mix and match napkins bought at yard sales and thrift stores for an eclectic look.

. . . .

Self-Serve

Buffets and family-style dinners are an easy way to serve a crowd and immediately say, "Make yourself at home." Guests can get the amount of food they want and avoid things they don't like. A buffet is also an ideal place to focus your decorating attention, so have fun with it! Use cake plates and pedestals to add height to the arrangement. Don't be afraid to incorporate elements of your decorating style. I like to use vintage scales and ironstone in many of my buffet setups.

Frugal Flowers

For years, my go-to tip for flowers was to get them at the grocery store. Although grocery stores are still cheaper than florists, they have gotten pretty expensive (in my opinion). So try using potted herbs and flowers that will last longer than fresh-cut flowers. Or cut some stems from your garden or—with permission—from an obliging field of wildflowers. Fresh fruit is also a nice stand-in for flowers.

Kids' Table

You can really have fun and make the kids' table a coveted place to sit. Fill a tote with cards, games, and crayons to encourage the kids to play and create. A roll of brown craft paper can make a disposable tablecloth and the perfect canvas for artwork. Avoid using anything delicate that would break if knocked over and flower arrangements filled with water that might be spilled in a spirited game of cards. Create a kids' menu that offers pint-sized portions of kiddie favorites like macaroni and cheese, chicken nuggets, and fruit.

Place Markers

There's something very inviting about place markers. They say, "I set this place just for you and put you next to people I thought you would enjoy." They show that forethought and attention were given to each guest. Clever place-card holders are readily available on sites like Etsy, but you can also find them in nature. Use double-sided tape to stick a small paper tag on the stem of a pear, or tuck the first initial of each guest's name in a pinecone.

Have fun with these ideas, and make them your own to fit both the occasion and your style of entertaining. Remember that the goal isn't to have perfection in all of the details but to enjoy your guests. If you're stressed-out, you just might miss out on that enjoyment.

Bed-and-Breakfast

It took a few years of living in my own home before I realized the importance of having a comfortable place for guests to stay. For too long, my guest room had received only leftovers and very little attention. I finally noticed my father-in-law bringing his own alarm clock and bedside lamp whenever he came to visit. That was a "duh" moment for me, and I took some time to make our guest room functional for those staying the night in our home.

Is your guest room comfortable? Try spending the night in it to see. Maybe the mattress is rock hard, the lighting isn't sufficient for reading in bed, and there's nowhere to put a suitcase. Think through guest rooms and hotels you've enjoyed staying in, and put together a list of what they have in common. Use that list to make your guest room a special place to stay.

It's All About the Bed

Nice hotels splurge on super-comfortable mattresses because they know it's all about the bed. Now, my family is going to laugh at this because we have a full-size bottom-of-the-line mattress in our guest room. It's just not in the budget to get a lush pillow top at this point, but I've done everything I can within my budget, and I've tested it out myself to make sure it passes. A layer of egg-crate foam, a cushy mattress pad, crisp white sheets, and feather pillows make it comfy. Always make sure extra blankets and pillows are available.

Leave Room

Make sure your guests have plenty of room to make themselves at home. Leave space for a suitcase, some room on a dresser, and a bit of real estate on the rod in

the closet. (Again, I hear my family chuckling. Excuse me. I need to go clean out my guest-room closet.)

Comforts of Home

Provide your guests with things you would want in your own room. Reading lights, bedside tables, an alarm clock, and a mirror are a few of the staples in a well-equipped guest room. It's also a good idea to keep on hand some extra toiletries like a contact-lens case, a new toothbrush, and sample bottles of shampoo in case one of your guests forgets something.

Shop the House

If you don't have a steady stream of guests year-round, shop the rest of your house for furniture, accessories, or lighting to use in your guest room while guests are staying there. Think outside of the box when doing this. A stack of vintage suitcases, a kitchen bar stool, or a pretty chair can all function as a side table in a pinch.

Mini Guest Room

I realize not everyone has the luxury of a spare bedroom. The lack of space shouldn't prevent you from setting up a cozy area for your guests to sleep. Use a daybed, sleeper sofa, air mattress, or cot to create a comfortable nook.

Keep It Neutral

I try to decorate my guest room so it feels gender neutral. I can't imagine my dad snuggling into a frilly pink bed that's exploding with lace pillows and teddy bears. Try to strike a balance between the masculine and feminine to create an environment that's comfortable for anyone who stays there.

Consider these other thoughtful guest room touches:

- A variety of reading materials, puzzles, games, and cards to offer some entertainment for your guests
- A selection of packaged snacks and a few bottles of water
- Brochures advertising things to do in the area

- A pitcher of freshly picked flowers
- An empty outlet for charging cell phones and laptops
- A note card sharing your Wi-Fi log-in and password information
- A devotional book
- An itinerary with addresses and phone numbers if guests are there for a special event
- "Welcome" cards handmade by your kids to include the little ones in the joys of hospitality

Use your hospitality to encourage everyone who enters your home, as well as those who live there, including you.

INSPIRED ENTERTAINING MADE EASY

The concept of hospitality is becoming more and more foreign in our society today. I'll be the first to admit I often make the excuse that I'm too busy to invite people over for dinner. I love entertaining, but I always seem to put it on the back burner. It's just easier not to do it. The truth is, though, entertaining isn't limited to having people over for dinner. You can find creative ways to fit hospitality into your busy life.

- Look for opportunities to share with those who are in need of food, fellowship, or help.
- Invite a few families from your neighborhood or church over for a potluck dinner in your home.
- Prepare a meal and deliver it to a family who is struggling or in need after an injury, accident, or surgery.
- Bake bread or cookies, and deliver them to your neighbors.
- Host a women's tea at your house, and invite ladies who don't know one another.
- Invite some students from a local college over for a home-cooked meal and the opportunity to do their laundry for free.
- Offer to host a small group, book club, or playgroup.
- If you have a green thumb, share your flowers and produce with people in need.

Keep in mind what is at the heart of hospitality—love. Any act of hospitality, no matter how big or small, will be appreciated by those on the receiving end of that action. Don't let an imperfect house, imperfect cooking, or an imperfect family prevent you from sharing that love with others. Some of the humblest forms of hospitality can also be the most impactful.

Whether you like entertaining with paper cups and takeout or fine china and fancy food, I hope you are inspired to use your hospitality to encourage everyone who enters your home, as well as those who live there, *including you*. We can find much joy in making our guests feel special, comfortable, and at home. Serving others is good for our hearts as well. I hope you will be on the giving and receiving ends of hospitality. Your life will be richly blessed because of it.

Chapter 9

FINDING
CONTENTMENT

I'VE TOLD JEFF BEFORE, "If ever I'm sitting quietly in a room, looking around, you can be almost certain that I'm redecorating the space in my mind." He has learned to recognize "the look" I get when I'm ready to share my latest idea for a project or when I'm about to pile more onto the honey-do list. I often hear a quiet groan when I start a conversation with "I was thinking . . ." He's right to groan, though, because my ideas usually involve rearranging furniture, filling the house with paint fumes, and shopping for the perfect item to finish off the room.

One day as I was rattling off some ideas, he interrupted me. "Is the house *ever* going to be finished?" His question stopped me in my tracks. Finished? I felt sweaty at even the thought of committing to a room being finished. I've always viewed the kind of person who *finishes* a room as someone who ends up with an avocado refrigerator in her kitchen thirty years after it was the "in look." I don't know if I ever

want to be finished. I like repainting walls and moving things around. Buying and selling furniture gives me the flexibility to keep one piece and sell another. Working on my home is one of my favorite pastimes, and I would be so bored in a house that didn't need some kind of work done.

I later realized that my husband wasn't asking me to commit to a specific decorating style, wall color, or furniture arrangement. His deeper question was "Will you ever be content?" I hadn't ever stopped to think that all my painting and repainting and rearranging and redecorating might be revealing a lack of contentment in my heart. I had to examine my motives and be honest with myself about some things.

Yes, I love decorating and all things home, and there's nothing wrong with that. I admit that I may be a bit of a weirdo because I really like painting. I love being productive, and that is displayed in the work I do on my home. It's my business and hobby rolled into one, so it's okay that I give a lot of attention to it. But it's also true that I can be really excited about a project I spent time and money on, and then a few weeks later I'm bored with it and want to make something new. And I can look at beautiful homes in magazines, books, and blogs and then feel like I want to redecorate my entire house . . . or buy a new

one. And at times I look at my house and, instead of noticing how richly blessed I am in so many ways, I just see what I don't have and what I still want. I've even found myself down in the dumps on days when my house is a real mess. My emotions are being dictated by the state of my house! That doesn't sound like contentment.

I SUFFER FROM SDAP (SHORT DECORATING ATTENTION SPAN)

A couple of years ago, I decided our master bedroom needed some decorating attention. It's a room I have always struggled with. It's long and narrow, has too many doorways, and has only one window that's smack in the middle of the wall where I believe the bed *should* go. Over the five-plus years we've lived here, I have stared at this room for hours and had many "I was thinking . . ." conversations with Jeff about it. So, after repainting the walls about eight times, I realized the wall color wasn't the issue. I needed to address the flow of the space.

I decided it would look great to have the bed against the far wall. The problem? There was a doorway to my office right where the headboard would be. *How can I cover that doorway?* I thought. I considered building a huge headboard or cladding the wall in wood paneling, but I eventually decided a fabric bed crown would make the bed a beautiful focal point *and* would cover the doorway without any major construction. (A bed crown is a half canopy that's attached to the ceiling.)

I went to the fabric store with my coupons and birthday money and splurged on about fifteen yards of fabric. I spent several hours sewing the panels together and stapling them to the board that would be attached to the ceiling. The excitement I felt about this bed crown had me certain this would be my greatest DIY achievement ever. I could hardly sit still waiting for it to be installed over our bed. I walked around the house, making it obvious that I wanted this bed crown to be hung as soon as there was a spare second and Jeff had the slightest inclination.

A day or two later, Jeff installed the bed crown and helped me move all the furniture. (I'm pretty sure I repainted the walls once more, just for good measure.) I was over the moon with joy. I snapped pictures of it and proudly posted about it on my blog. When I settled into bed that night, I swore our mattress was more comfortable under the beautiful bed crown. I knew I would love it forever. (Can you guess what's coming next?)

Not even a year later, I started staring at the bed crown, wishing I had picked a different fabric or that I had gone with the wood paneling idea. I waited for the perfect moment to casually say to Jeff, "I was thinking about taking down that bed crown and covering the doorway with something else." When I finally mustered the courage to reveal my new plan to him, I received the expected reply. Jeff pointed out that I had been near tears with joy and love over that bed crown. Less than a year later, I wanted to take it down? Yes, I did. I was done with it. My love had waned.

I joke about suffering from a short decorating attention span, but the truth is that discontentment is probably at the heart of a lot of those changes. I'll be happy with my room if I can only do fill-in-the-blank to it. There's a problem when my happiness is based on how I feel about the decor in my house. It means tear-inducing-joy-over-a-bed-crown one minute and bummed-that-my-husband-(wisely)-won't-let-me-take-down-said-bed-crown-this-instant-because-I'm-done-with-it the next. It's not wrong for us to want to change things in our homes to our

> *There's a problem when my happiness is based on how I feel about the decor in my house.*

evolving tastes, but it can become unhealthy when we're too emotionally invested in it and we forget that stuff is just stuff.

I WANT THAT!

When Marshall was almost five, I felt he was old enough to look through a toy catalog and tell me what he wanted for Christmas. We sprawled out on the floor together, and I explained to him that Christmas was coming soon, so he could look through this magazine and show me things he liked. I opened the colorful catalog, and his eyes lit up. "Oh, Mommy! I want this!" Score! I was so happy that right off the bat he found something he was excited about. I made a mental note of the choice as he kept looking over the page. "And I want this, this, this, this, and that. Oh, and that too." He pointed to everything on the page. I started to think, *This kid is going to be very disappointed on Christmas morning if we continue.* So I closed the catalog and went about my Christmas shopping another way.

> *If we find ourselves constantly wishing for and wanting more, perhaps we need to close the catalog and focus on all the things we have to be thankful for.*

Isn't that how we all are, though? We'll go through life pointing at everything, saying, "I want that!"—and there's a lot of stuff to point to. We live in a society where we are bombarded with the message that we need to *have* more and *be* more. It's in our faces, it's in subliminal messages, and it's available 24/7 in the palms of our hands and at the touch of a button. The truth is, I was

probably much more content with my home before I started writing my blog and browsing Pinterest. When I began looking constantly at the clever ideas and beautiful rooms shared on other blogs, I felt compelled to make everything in my own home better and better. I thought I had to compete with all of the perfectly staged, Photoshopped pictures of beautiful homes in magazines and on other blogs. I would seriously say things like, "We would have a great kitchen if I could repaint the cabinets, replace the counters, build a cool range hood, install new flooring, get new hardware, paint the walls, replace the sink and faucet, and get all new appliances. *Then* it would be perfect. *Then* it would be magazine-worthy." How ridiculous (and expensive) is that list?

It's our nature to see things and desire them. People have been struggling with it since God created the world. If we continue to crave the next best thing, though, we'll never find contentment. If we find ourselves constantly wishing for and wanting more, perhaps we need to close the catalog and focus on all the things we have to be thankful for. There's no better way to readjust our perspective and move to a place where "I want that!" is referring to kindness, love, humility, and contentment.

PRACTICING CONTENTMENT

When our focus is on being thankful, earthly treasures start to lose their importance. Suddenly our wish lists shrink, and we're a lot more appreciative of what we have. That doesn't mean we all move into cardboard boxes and start wearing potato sacks. The problem isn't in what we own or how much of it we have but in how we view those possessions.

We can find many ways to nurture contentment in our own lives, which can then be an example to our children and others around us. To be able to say that we are content no matter the circumstance is definitely a treasure that has great worth. So, what are some practical ways we can find contentment in our lives and in our homes?

Be Thankful

If you struggle with being thankful, expand your horizons. I went on a mission trip to Russia when I was a teenager, and it had a profound effect on me. I met children who only had gum wrappers as toys and mothers who had to cook meals for their families with what little food they had. Despite their poverty, they were generous and thankful. I'm often reminded of my summer spent there without a washing machine and clean drinking water, and it puts things into proper perspective when I'm wishing for new countertops or wanting to remodel a perfectly adequate bathroom.

- Be thankful for everything in your life, even trials. We often grow the most in times of want and hardship.
- Turn complaints into gratitude: "I'm so thankful that pipe burst in my bathroom. It's giving me a perfect opportunity to practice patience and self-control." (Easier said than done, I know!)

Serve

You don't have to travel halfway around the world to gain a proper perspective on your possessions. You can serve those less fortunate who are in your own backyard. Serving others brings joy that far outlasts any high attained from retail therapy.

- Volunteer at your church, a homeless shelter, a mission, or a school. Be sure to find a program that uses your gifts and abilities.
- Offer to help people who are moving or making home improvements.
- Cook a meal and take it to someone in need.

Give Generously

Someone, somewhere, always has less than you do. Sharing what you have with others is a great way to combat selfishness. Remember that giving isn't always about writing a check. You can give your time, gifts, talents, and resources as well.

- Have a yard sale and donate the proceeds to a ministry, church, or charity.
- Save your pocket change and give it to a family in need at the end of each month.
- Offer to spend time with patients in a hospital or retirement home.
- Make something to give away to others.

Sheet-Music Wreath Tutorial

I spotted a version of a paper wreath on a blog a few years ago and immediately knew I wanted to make one out of antique sheet music. This high-impact, low-cost project is easy to make and great to give away. So make two—one for yourself and one to give to someone else. I would also encourage you to give it to someone who wouldn't expect it. Tell your mom you'll make her one later (because she will want one!).

What you'll need:

- Cardboard
- Pencil
- Scissors
- Cream grosgrain ribbon

- Hot glue gun
- Hot glue sticks
- Sheet music (or you can use book pages)

Step 1: Create Cardboard Wreath Form

Step 1

Cut a circle with about a 12-inch diameter out of a piece of stiff cardboard. Use a large bowl or bucket as a template if needed. The form will not be visible, so it doesn't matter if the circle is perfect. Use the scissors to punch a hole in the center of the circle and cut a smaller, 4-inch-wide circle out of the middle. (I often used the side of a diaper box for these, so just use whatever cardboard you have on hand.)

Step 2: Attach Ribbon

Cut a length of grosgrain ribbon about 2½ feet long. Apply a dab of hot glue near the edge of the cardboard wreath form. Press one end of ribbon in the hot glue and hold in place. Apply a second dab of hot glue on top of the ribbon and press the other end in place. Hold until glue cools.

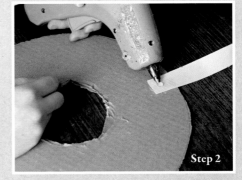
Step 2

Step 3

Step 3

Step 3: Roll and Glue Sheet Music

Place a piece of sheet music on the work surface. Turn it so it's horizontal. Put your left index finger at the center point of the paper and use your right hand to lift the right side of the piece of paper. Start to roll it over on itself. Continue to roll the piece of paper until a cone is formed. Apply a dab of hot glue on the corner of the sheet music and press into place. Allow glue to cool. Situate the wreath so the ribbon is at top and facing up. Apply a bead of hot glue and stick the cone to it so that the point is going toward the center of the wreath. Make a second cone and glue it to the bottom, again with the point of the cone facing in. Repeat on the left and right sides. Starting in a north, south, east, west pattern will ensure the wreath looks even when it's hung. Make more cones, and fill in the spaces between the four glued cones until the entire cardboard form is covered. Then create a second layer of full-sized sheet-music cones.

Step 4: Roll and Glue Last Layer

Use a sharp pair of scissors or a paper cutter to cut several pieces of sheet music in half. Roll them as you did the larger ones and use them to create a third inside layer of the wreath. Fill in with cones until you have achieved the desired look. Clean up the glue strings, and the wreath is ready to hang.

• *If you're using antique sheet music, make sure it's still pliable. Some aged paper will become brittle and can no longer be rolled.*

• *When gluing the cones to the wreath form, change the angle of the point slightly for each one to achieve a random, fluffy look around the edges.*

• *Sheet music that is very busy, such as pieces for orchestras or piano, is my preference.*

• *Small sheet-music wreaths can be made to use as ornaments on a Christmas tree. Glue the cones to a small cardboard circle and have all points meet in the middle. Use 8 1/2-by-11-inch sheets of paper that are cut into quarters and eighths so that the scale is right.*

THE DAILY CHOICE TO BE CONTENT

Back to the question Jeff posed: "Is the house *ever* going to be finished?" I have to laugh and say that the answer to that question is probably no. I love all aspects of decorating. It's one of my love languages and a way I care for my family. My home is also a hangout for teenagers, and we've used it for hosting small groups and dinners. I can't ever imagine not having a project list. There may be a time when my "nesting" goes away and I'm led in a different direction, but until that day, I doubt I'll consider the house finished. Sorry, Jeff!

> *I am much happier (and so is my family) when I'm not consumed with my wish list.*

But my answer to the more important question—*Will I ever be content?*—is yes. It's something I have to choose daily. I know there will be moments when I'll get a bee in my bonnet about replacing our countertops or I'll grumble because I have white appliances and not stainless steel. In those times, I have to stop focusing on everything I want and focus on what I have. I'm not saying that getting to a place of complete contentment is easy, but I know that I am much happier (and so is my family) when I'm not consumed with my wish list.

If you've struggled to find contentment as I have, you don't have to wallow in your past shortcomings. We've all had those moments when we're in a funk because we feel like we should have hardwood floors instead of the beige carpet the previous owners installed that is now spotted with stains. (Can you tell I've had those moments?) But even on bad days with bad carpet, we can set our sights on the things that really matter—such as friendship, family, and faith—and live our lives with a spirit of contentment.

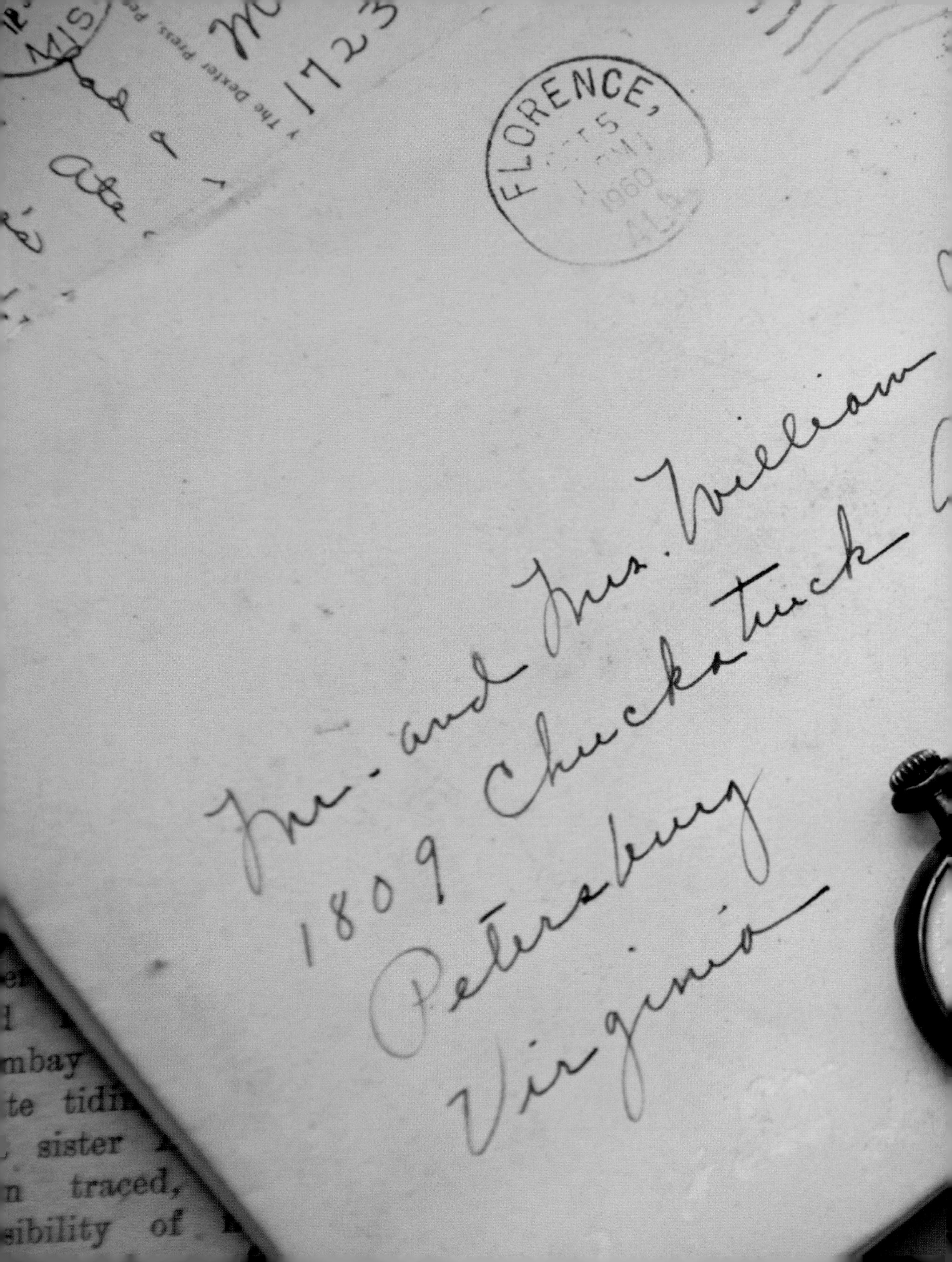

Mr. and Mrs. William

1809 Chuckatuck

Petersburg

Virginia

Chapter 10

IF WALLS
COULD TALK

WHAT MEMORIES COME TO MIND when you hear the word *home*? Perhaps you see images of warmth, comfort, love, safety, family, and tradition. You may remember specific instances of sliding down a banister on Christmas morning or the smell of freshly cut grass wafting in through an open window on a beautiful spring day. Maybe you recall how awesome it is to be home again after an extended time away. For me, *home* means memories of sitting on the porch during a rainstorm, sleeping under the quilt my mom made for me, and playing hide-and-seek in the attic. Or it's thoughts of the first home Jeff and I bought. Our bathtub leaked the day we moved in, and water was running down the kitchen and family room walls. It was hard not to laugh (and cry a little) at the realistic welcome to homeownership.

What does your home say about you right now?

There is a strong connection between the physical homes we make and the life and memories that are built within them. Creating a home is about so much more than the process and the end result; it's about the effects on the people who live there. And believe it or not, the decorating style used in a home can have a great impact on the kind of memories made there. Is the home gloomy or neglected? Is there plastic on the furniture and ropes across rooms that aren't supposed to be used? Is it quirky, fun, and playful? Is it chic and stylish? When you're in your home, how does it make you feel? Stressed, distracted, or depressed? Inspired, comfortable, or proud? How do you *want* it to feel?

If the style of our homes can impact our lives and the memories created along the way, we may want to make sure that the style we choose mirrors the personalities and needs of those who live there. So, what does your home say about you right now? Is it an accurate reflection of you and your family? Is it a place that will nurture fond memories of home? What do you *want* your home to say about you?

FINDING YOUR STYLE

Perhaps you've tried some of the projects and decorating ideas in this book, your creativity has been sparked, you're inspired, and you're ready to do more. But maybe you're struggling with even knowing what you like. Maybe you know what you want your home to say, but you're not sure how to translate that message into a style. How can you create a home you love when you don't really know what you love? You find yourself over the moon for industrial-chic one minute, but then you sway toward midcentury-modern the next. Instead of your home reflecting your personality, you have to write an essay to accurately describe the style displayed in your house: "It's transitional-French-bohemian-country-log-cabin-chic-cottage-junk-style." If you feel as if you need to add the words ". . . but it's not really *me*" to the end of that essay, it's time to find your style.

Do Your Research

When you're looking for style inspiration, here's the question you have to ask yourself: *Do I love this style, or do I love this style for* my home? *Does this style capture the way I want my home to feel?* Start an inspiration notebook or file to collect magazine clippings or digital images of spaces and rooms you love. Once you have a good collection, sort through them to find common elements. You should be able to see similarities that tie them all together. Start to base your decorating choices on that common thread.

Don't Try to Fit in a Box

Your style does not have to be easily categorized or labeled. It's okay if you like to mix coastal with cabin, cottage with country, modern with medieval. You don't have to justify your space or style to anyone else. Just do what works for you and your family, and throw decorating convention out the window.

. . . .

Tip: If you have trouble breaking out of a rigid style box you've put yourself in, try bringing in one element from a contrasting or complementary style. For example, give a Queen Anne dining set an entirely new look by pairing the table with some quirky modern chairs, or swap out the table for a rustic harvest one. Finding that unique blend of styles can be fun and will reward you with a home that's completely "you."

. . . .

Remember—It's Your Style

If you really love mauve and blue with a teddy bear border, and everyone else is ripping it down and talking about how hideously dated that is, don't let that sway you. Declare your love for 1980s decor from the rooftop, and take the opinions of others with a grain of salt. It's your home, and you need to be comfortable in it.

MAKING TIMELESS DECORATING CHOICES

Once you discover your style, how can you decorate in a way that won't look dated in five or ten years? It's always nice to make updates and changes here and there, but it's not very practical or budget friendly to overhaul the entire house on a regular basis. Here are some tips to making choices that will stand the test of time.

Know Your Staples

I'm sure there are things you have in your home that you have loved for years. Maybe it's a color, a detail, one piece of furniture, a collection, a fabric, or a pattern. Maybe it's just one accessory. Some of my staples are antiques, blue and white, ironstone, dark woods, and French provincial. I have loved and used all of these for more than ten years, and I have never grown tired of them. Put a list together of your staples, and work your decorating around those elements.

Determine Fad vs. Forever

Look through dated magazines or home decor books. I'm talking overstuffed furniture, baskets hung everywhere, dried flowers, and geese. Look past the big bangs, high-gloss brass hardware, and overabundance of froof, and see what is in the room that would look awesome in a home today. It may be classic pieces of furniture, neutral fabrics, or color combinations that have been around for centuries. You'll be

surprised at how much would still look great. This realization will give you a good clue for what is fad and what is timeless. Spend your decorating dollars on the latter and buy the former for less, knowing it will change.

Don't Muddy the Decorating Waters

I should say *try* not to muddy the decorating waters—we all allow things in our homes that we don't love or even like, especially those of us on a tight budget. We accept freebies or buy a $5 sofa that doesn't complement anything else we have, and those pieces make it hard for us (or anyone else) to see what our style is. The mammoth 1970s hutch from Aunt Beverly or the orange burlap recliner you picked up off the curb doesn't speak to the airy coastal look you're after. I'm not saying to chuck it all today, but just know those pieces are temporary, and don't buy pillows that coordinate with the recliner or the dining set that matches the hutch. Be patient and only add pieces that are "you."

Take Your Time

Don't make big, drastic decorating decisions quickly. You may decide one afternoon that you are totally in love with a superbusy wallpaper and immediately hang it on every wall in your house. Two months later, you have to swallow your pride and have an "I was thinking . . ." conversation with your spouse about

Remember the goal you're working toward: home. A home whose walls and rooms tell the story of the family who lives there.

taking down all of the wallpaper because it was a mistake. You'll save yourself a lot of time, money, and pride-swallowing conversations if you take your time.

THE GOAL

I'm excited for you as you embark on the journey to discover (or refine) your style, unearth (or dust off) hidden talents, and continue to learn new DIY skills. I wish I could join you on your secondhand shopping trips or be there when you unveil your first piece of repainted furniture to your friends and family. I also want to be there when the journey is hard and you're frustrated by tight budgets and time constraints. There will be times when you'll want to scream and chuck your sewing machine out the window. You'll make mistakes (because we all do), and there will be tears (because sometimes you just need a good cry during a DIY project). But through the ups and downs of your journey, remember that you're in good company. With all the successes I've had over the last few

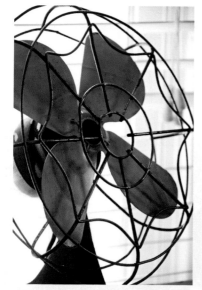 years, I've also had my share of failures (and tears).

But I know you're ready to tackle the obstacles that are in your way. And on the days when you're not sure if you are, remember the goal you're working toward: home. Not a perfect home. Not an "impress the neighbors" home. Just home. A home that was made, not bought. A home whose walls and rooms tell the story of the family who lives there.

My Dear Sister Kerr,

Remembering, th[at]
will have reached the One Hundredth Mile Stone
I wish to Congratulate you on the Signal M[ercies?]
Goodness which has permitted you to reach such [a]
to enjoy so many of life's blessings and opportun[ities]
your Children, and numerous friends, in giving [you]
Most Sincere thanks, for what you have been to [me?]
and to all, who have known and loved you.

Have you forgotten that I was one [who?]
at the Session of the Virginia Conference in Petersbu[rg]
just a little more than forty one years ago? I[?]
homes and pleasant Entertainments since then, but
do that; and one that, in the retrospect of my Mind
with so much pleasure. What a happy home was y[ours]
and Elegant Hospitality you dispensed! For good [and?]
Servants, your Companionship, bright and attract[ive]
[?], Sincere unostentatious [?] and loving
[?] of [?] Excelled in Virg[inia]
[?] fall of 1862 I was appointed
of Ho[?] which made me your pastor & th[e]
The [?] war was then in progress, and soon
[?] disposing [?]ies. There was no parsonage for m[e]
but poorly [?]ed to receive and provide for [me?]
[?] it into your heart [?] give us welcome to your home
your roof we found [?] and many Comforts, a[nd]
Wife and I love to talk [?] those days, and to think

During your journey, remember . . .

- There is an inspired version of yourself just waiting to be discovered.
- You don't need to make your home perfect—just perfect for your family.
- Even magazine homes aren't magazine homes all the time.
- Find value in things others do not.
- Even the broken can be made new.
- A beautiful home is made one project at a time.
- High style can be created on a low budget.
- The heart of hospitality is love.
- Stuff is just stuff.
- Your home makes a statement about you. What do you want it to say?

My journey started with hand painting some ornaments and refinishing a dresser. The decision to take some action in my life and to use my home as a place to exercise the gifts and resources God had given me has exploded into so much more. Your journey may start with making a wreath, setting a table, upholstering a headboard, or building an ottoman. And you just never know where it will lead you and how God will use it to richly bless your life and touch your heart.

*Hopefully you'll create an **inviting home** for your family,*

*you'll find **increasing joy**,*

*and you'll discover the **inspired you**.*

....

For more encouragement, ideas, and inspiration, visit Miss Mustard Seed on her blog at www.missmustardseed.com.

....

And be sure to try Miss Mustard Seed's new line of milk paint!

For a list of retailers and additional information, visit www.missmustardseedsmilkpaint.com.